T. E. Brown

An Anthology

T. E. Brown
1830 - 1897

T. E. Brown
An Anthology

Selected and introduced by Dollin Kelly
Illustrated by Catherine James

Published by the Manx Heritage Foundation, P.O. Box 1986,
Douglas, Isle of Man.

First published 1997

ISBN No 0 952 4019 2 4

Layout and typesetting by The Manx Heritage Foundation
Cover design by Ruth Sutherland
Latin translations by Revd. R. L. Thomson
Photograph of T. E. Brown by G. B. Cowen of Ramsey
Photographs courtesy of Manx National Heritage

Printed by Mannin Printing, Douglas

Introduction

T. E. Brown is rightly known as The Manx National Poet, not only because he wrote about the Isle of Man but also because his poems were published in England and distributed throughout the world. Amongst his works which appeared in print was a "collected" edition of his poems, published by Macmillan after his death, in the same series as the widely-read works of Tennyson, Wordsworth, Shelley and other mainstream English poets.

His poems, though, should not be remembered, learned and recited simply because he was a Manxman but because they are true poems. Many are written in established forms, such as sonnets but for the *Fo'c's'le Yarns* Brown has invented his own form with four stressed syllables in each line and an irregular number of unstressed ones to balance them; this form he termed "asynartate octosyllables". Unlike the words thrown together by other Island residents both then and since, and described as poetry just because they rhyme, his works were the product of a trained, classical mind and they have imagery and emotion which reveal their author's deep and sympathetic nature.

Thomas Edward Brown was born the sixth of ten children, on the 5th of May 1830 to Dorothy, wife of the Reverend Robert Brown. Robert was a poor and overworked clergyman who held the combined post of chaplain to St. Matthew's Church and Master of Douglas Grammar School. The family home was in New Bond Street in the poorest, dirtiest and most unhygienic part of the town. It was demolished in 1934 as part of the slum clearances.

The year of Brown's birth was an auspicious one for the Island as the Isle of Man Steam Packet Company commenced trading then and the foundation stone for King William's College was finally laid after more than a hundred years of argument. Both these events caused tremendous change in the Island and Brown was very keen to record the disappearing Island scenes in his "local" poems so that future generations might have an idea of the old ways of life which were rapidly passing away.

South and West Douglas in those days were in the parish of Braddan. The rest of Douglas was in Onchan parish. In 1832 Robert Brown was appointed curate of Braddan and the family moved there. This was the year of the great cholera epidemic when thousands of Manx people died. Luckily the Browns escaped its ravages and T. E. Brown grew up learning the ways of the countryside and meeting mainly country people. The children went to school at Port-y-Shee but their father, who was appointed vicar in 1834, was a poet and musician and a very scholarly man. It was he who taught the children to appreciate good literature as well as History, Latin and Greek. When Thomas was sixteen, his father died and the family moved to live with an aunt in Castletown. Thomas went to King William's College as a day boy. He was very fond of walking in out of school hours and it was possibly then, "knocking about in boats" and mixing with seafarers in Derbyhaven, Castletown, Port Erin and Port St. Mary that he learned to love the sea.

His scholarship to Oxford took the form of a servitorship at Christ's College. He didn't actually have to serve the other students but the servitors were humiliated by a system which kept them apart from the other men, had them wear different gowns and eat their meals at different times and even kept them apart in chapel. Despite the very bitter feelings implanted by this system, Brown obtained a "Double First" in Classics and Modern History and he was elected a Fellow of Oxford's premier college - Oriel.

After a spell as an Oxford tutor, he returned to the Island in 1856 as Vice-Principal of King William's College and he married his second cousin, Amelia Stowell, at Maughold, the following year. They left the Island in 1861 when Brown was appointed Head of The Crypt School in Gloucester but he managed to fall foul of the parents and the public there and by 1864 he was Second Master (Vice-Principal) and Head of Moderns at the newly opened Clifton College at Bristol. Here he remained for the rest of his teaching career. He and Amelia had six children; the eldest, Amy Dora was aged only three months when she died in August 1858 and was buried in Maughold Churchyard and a son, Braddan, died of diptheria when he was seven. He was buried at Clifton, as was his mother who died in 1888. Brown had loved Amelia deeply and his health was never good after she died. He retired to live in Ramsey in 1891 and spent his time reading, letter writing, walking and lecturing. He holidayed off the Island quite frequently and was giving a talk to the boys at Clifton when he suffered a brain haemorrhage and died on the 29th October, 1897. He was buried in the same grave as Braddan and Amelia.

Although several prose articles of Brown's had been published, it was not until 1872 that his first poem appeared in print. This was *Betsy Lee*, the first of twelve *Fo'c's'le Yarns* which were finally published as one work in the Golden Treasury series in 1881. Being written in the Anglo-Manx dialect, they were not widely read nor very easily understood but they were tremendously well received by fellow authors, poets and even critics. They have given us a lasting picture of the way of life for ordinary Manx people in the early nineteenth century and Brown was able to reach a wider audience eventually when his book Old John and Other Poems, written in normal English, was published to general acclaim in 1893.

T. E. Brown, An Anthology has been compiled to mark the centenary of Brown's death. The Manx Heritage Foundation is donating copies to Island schools in the hope that young people will be introduced to our national poet's works. It hopes that the general public will welcome the book as well. Much of what Brown wrote is now archaic or assumes a specialised knowledge; and rather than have footnotes which interfere with the flow of the poetry and a glossary at the back of the book, we have provided 'notes' and 'words' before each poem. However, despite the locations and events being old-fashioned, human nature does not seem to have changed at all and the deep humanity of the poet and his love for his fellow man stand out in every line.

It is almost certain that if you read these poems you will enjoy them and gain from the experience; we hope so, and we hope it will lead to many of you reading more of Brown's works in, perhaps *The Collected Poems of T. E. Brown* which, at the time of writing is still readily available in a facsimile, hardback edition.

Dollin Kelly, October 1997.

Contents

Lyrical Poems:

Brown's Birthplace, New Bond Street
The Schoolmaster's house is on the left (with the porch)
and the Grammar School continues beyond.
It was demolished in 1934 and the site is now occupied by the bus
terminal. The exact location of the Grammar School is near to Bay
5 on the north side of the terminal building.

FOREWORD

The Manx Heritage Foundation is pleased to be undertaking a reassessment of the work of the Island's national poet, T. E. Brown.

Since the centenary celebrations of his birth in 1930, when every Island school was given a large portrait of Brown to create an awareness of his status as the Manx National Poet, his broad popularity has gradually decreased, and apart from one or two famous poems and occasional performances of extracts from his fo'c's'le yarns, he is not accorded the popularity he once enjoyed. This is partly due to fashion, and partly due to the fact that many of the concepts and even the language that he used now seem remote from us at the end of the 20th century.

As 1997 is the centenary of his death, the Manx Heritage Foundation felt it was time to publish a new selection of his works, and to look at them in a fresh light. We were delighted that Dollin Kelly, one of the leading exponents of Brown's dialect poetry, agreed to undertake the task of selecting the poems and writing informative background notes to them, thereby giving us the context in which they were written and an idea of the influences that made Brown the man he was.

The feeling of a Victorian Isle of Man has been greatly enhanced in this book by the superb pencil sketches of Catherine James, who has caught the essence of the atmosphere created by the words.

The Manx Heritage Foundation hopes that this new selection of T. E. Brown's poetry will find a place on the shelves of many Manx homes and be used in Island schools and will bring to the attention of new generations of Manx people the very real value of the Island's only true National Poet.

Hon. N. Q. Cringle SHK.,
Chairman, Manx Heritage Foundation

DIALECT POEMS

T. E. Brown was born in 1830, the year the Isle of Man Steam Packet Company began trading and the early tourist industry was starting in the Island. Most of his poems are written in MANX DIALECT which is the way Manx working people spoke English at that time when the native Manx Gaelic (Gaelg) was dying out.

Brown was very keen to let future generations know some of the stories from those times and to spell the words in a way which would help us know what the people's talking sounded like.

He wrote the next two poems to explain his reasons.

DEDICATION
(Fo'c'sle Yarns, first series**)**

To sing a song shall please my countrymen;
To unlock the treasures of the Island heart;
With loving feet to trace each hill and glen,
And find the ore that is not for the mart
Of commerce: this is all I ask.
No task,
But joy, GOD wot!
Wherewith "the stranger" intermeddles not—

Who, if perchance
He lend his ear,
As caught by mere romance
Of nature, traversing
On viewless wing
All parallels of sect
And race and dialect,
Then shall he be to me most dear.

Natheless, for mine own people do I sing,
And use the old familiar speech:
Happy if I shall reach
Their inmost consciousness.
One thing They will confess:
I never did them wrong,
And so accept the singer and the song.

DEDICATION
(Fo'c'sle Yarns, second series)

Dear Countrymen, whate'er is left to us
  Of ancient heritage—
  Of manners, speech, of humours, polity,
  The limited horizon of our stage—
  Old love, hope, fear,
  All this I fain would fix upon the page;
  That so the coming age,
     Lost in the empire's mass,
  Yet haply longing for their fathers, here
     May see, as in a glass,
  What they held dear—
May say, "'Twas thus and thus
  They lived"; and, as the time-flood onwards rolls,
  Secure an anchor for their Keltic souls.

THE CHRISTENING

What an understanding of human nature is shown in this poem. The father, Edward Creer, is so proud and excited at having a robust son and heir. He's been away at sea and feels guilty that he wasn't at home to comfort Kitty at the time of the birth - not that men were ever present in those days during the actual birth as they are now.

Delivering babies was definitely left to the women folk but now that the baby has arrived, "Eddart" takes charge. He sees that the boat is moored in the inner harbour so the crew can relax about its safety and celebrate the baby's safe arrival by drinking every drop of alcohol which can be found.

Words: fess=fist; **hess**=has; **my gough**=an acceptable way of saying **My God** (which is a blasphemy); **yandhar**=yonder; **bogh**=poor darling; **calkerlated**=calculated; **tuk**=took (Kitty took to her bed to have the baby); **close hauled**=sails tightly trimmed as a boat sails into the wind; **leeward** (loo'urd)=side which is sheltered from the wind; **All the kit**=the whole lot; **shiff**=baby's shift or shirt; **driff**=spindrift blown off the top of waves; **regard**=notice; **ess**=is; **warp her**=stand on the quayside and move the boat by pulling on the ropes (warps).
See also: Going to meet him (p.39); Mater Dolorossa (p.112).

THE CHRISTENING

Hould him up!
Hould him up!
Joy! Joy!
Hould him up! hould him up!
Is that the boy?
Hould him up!

 Stand out of the way, women,
Stand out of the way!
Here, Misthress Shimmin!
Here, I say!
Here! here!
Aw dear!
Is this him?

Every limb
Taut and trim—
Here's a hull!
Here's a breast—
Like a bull!
He's got my finger in his fess—
He hess! he hess!

    Look at the grip!
Is that a smile upon his lip?
He can't do that!
What! what!
Smile!
My gough! what a chile!

Feel the gristle!
Feel it though!
Stop! I'll whistle—
Whew—! bo!
What's he doin'?
Is it cooin'
You call it when he goes like yandhar?
See his eyes the way they wandhar!
Hullo! hullo!
Where'll you go? where'll you go?
Keep her so!

    There's a look!
There's another!
The little rook!
What's he wantin'
With this gallivantin'?
Ah! the mother! ah! the mother!
Yiss! yiss! muss hev a kiss!
Aw, Kitty, Kitty bogh!
Aw my gough!
Kitty darlin'! Kitty then!

And me so far away!
The hard it muss ha' ben!
Were you freckened, Kitty, eh?
Navar mind!
Here I am!
As consigned!
And, axin' your pardon, Misthress Shimmin,
     ma'am,
Here's the joy!
Here's our boy, Kitty!
Here's our boy!

    Listen! I'll tell you a thing—
By jing!
I've calkerlated it to a dot,
But whether or not—
The very night Kitty was tuk—
Just three days,
If you plaze,
Out of Dantzic, there was a sea struck—
Jemmy'll remember—
Every timber
Shuck!

Close-hauled, you know, and I tould ye,
But behould ye!
In the trough there, rowlin' in it,
Just that minute—
I saw a baby, as plain,
Passin' by on a slant of rain
To leeward, and his little shiff
Streamin' away in the long gray driff.
I saw him there—you didn' regard me—
But his face was toward me—
Oughtn't I to know him?
Well, I saw him afore Kitty saw him!
I saw him, and there he ess,

There upon his mother's breast,
The very same, I'll assure ye!
And I think that'll floor ye!
And his body all in a blaze of light—
A dirty night!
"Where was he goin'?"
Who's knowin'?
He was in a hurry in any case,
And the Baltic is a lonesome place—
But here he is, all right!
Here he is now! joy! joy!
God bless the boy!
Have you tould the Pazon? what did he say?
Has he seen him—ould Pazon Gale?
Aw, you tould the Pazon anyway!
Tould! he'll turn the scale
At thirty pound,
I'll be bound.

Did you put it in the papers?
No, no! What capers!
No, no!
Splendid though!
Upon my life—
Catharine, wife
Of Mounseer
Eddard Creer,
Esqueer,
Otherwise dadaa
Of a son and heer!
Hip-hip-hip-hip, hooraa!

    Bless my sowl! am I draemin'?
He'll make a seaman
Will yandhar lad—
Aw, the glad!
Yiss! yiss! Misthress Shimmin, certainly!

Go down to the smack,
Jemmy, and see—
Yiss! Misthress Shimmin
And all the rest of the women—
'Scuse me, ladies! rather 'cited—
Just the delighted, you know, the delighted!
And every raison to suppose
(See him cockin' his nose!)
That the best of care
And ceterar—
I'll get that with Misthress Shimmin—did ye say?
Eh?

Go, Jemmy, they're lyin' quite handy,
A bottle of rum and another of brandy,
In the starboard locker theer—
And, Jemmy! there's a taste of gin—
Aw, navar fear!
Tell the chaps to finish it—
All the kit—
And listen—tell ould Harper
We'll take and warp her
Inside
On the morning's tide—
About half-past four'll be time to begin—
My gough! but we'll have a chrizzenin'!

19

PEGGY'S WEDDING

Dan Cowle is similar to the whining man in Conjergal Rights. *Peggy, a servant, discovers on the way to her new home on her wedding night that he is not quite the lovely man she and her mistress had thought he was.*

We must realise when reading this poem that few working women travelled very far from home in bygone times and that the newly married Peggy, like dozens of other brides, travelled in a "horse and cart" to a home she had never seen.

Words: hommerin=hammering (at the door); **perricut**=petticoat; **slut**="chit" of a girl (not always a term of abuse); **halfway-house**=pub halfway between two towns; **trouse**=a slattern or trollop; **bellows**=implement for blowing on embers to start or re-start a coal or peat fire; **agen**=against; **concatenation**=linking together; **gradjal**=gradual; **gintale**=genteel; **ould pump-handle**=comparing Dan's unbending arm with the iron handle of a farmyard water pump; **seerchin**=searching; **rummin**=rum one; **puss**=purse; **crock**=a large earthenware jar; **priddha**=potato; **gor**=got; **war'**=table ware; **turmits**=turnips; **could**(cowled)=cold; **rot-hole**=rat-hole or, maybe, this <u>is</u> a hole caused by rotting; **shot-hole**=a hole for filling with explosive prior to blasting; **etha**=either; **male**=meal; **medha**=small, one-handled tub; **"scraas"** (scrairs) =peat strips laid on the rafters under the thatch; **harry-long-legses**=daddy-long-legs; **troof**=truth.

See also: Conjergal Rights (p.30).

PEGGY'S WEDDING

"Is that you, Peggy? my goodness me!
And so dark still I can hardly see!
Wait, woman, wait!
I'll come down: ye needn' go on hommerin'at such a rate.
Here's the master snorin'
Like a mill, and you to be breakin' the door in—
It's just disthractin,' that's what it is—
Aisy, woman! yis! yis!—
There's people'll snore—where's that perricut?
There's people'll hommer—my gough! that slut!
I'm comin'! I'm comin'!
God bless the woman!
I navar heard such a row—

"Aw dear! aw dear! aw, the craythur! aw, poor Peggy,
   what's the matter with you now?
Come in! come in! the sowl! the sowl!
What is it, Peggy, what? and where have you left Dan
   Cowle?
Is he outside in the street?—well, where is he then?
Did you call at the halfway-house? did he get—aw, bless
   these men!
Did he fall on the road! *No, ye say, no?*
Well then where did he go?
Is he lyin' in the ditch?
Did he lave you, or did you lave him—which?
You left *him?*
So I suppose it's not a man you're wantin'at all, but a
   cherubim?
Aye! aye!
Middlin' high!

   "And you that were married only yesterday, and the
      weddin' out of this house—
To be comin' a home in the mornin' all ragg'd and rumpled
   like a reg'lar trouse—
Peggy, Peggy! *You'd like to blow the fire, just to feel*
You're at home again—eh, Peggy? Don't kneel! don't kneel!
Don't be foolish, Peggy. There! take the bellows,
And blow away!
And we'll have a cup o'tay,
And then you'll tell us.
Why—Dan Cowle! Dan Ballabroo!
A dacent man, and well-to-do!
Dan! Dan Cowle! dear heart!
And the beautiful ye went away in the cart!
And you've tuk and left him! left Dan!
Left the man!"

   "*Man!* did ye say? aw Misthriss, Misthriss! what are ye
      talkin'?

Man! do ye call that craythur a man, because he's a thing
    that's walkin'
On two legs, and a tongue in his head? a beautiful surt
Of a man—you call him a man, I call him a dirt!
That's what I call him—a dirt, and a sneak and a dunkey—
Man! if that chap's a man, he's a cross' twix a man and a
    monkey!
And a touch of a divil, and a touch of a fool . . .
Listen, Misthriss, listen! We warn' half-way up Barrule,
When I thought he'd ha' stayed a bit—and only raisonable
    he shud—
At Kinvigs's—bein' a thing lek that's general understood—
What's halfway-houses for, I'd like to know—
Just so!
You wouldn' be agen that?
What?

    "Certainly! and company waitin'—and just a drop to warm
    a body—
And dear me! what is there in half a glass of rum, or a whole
    glass, for the matter of that, to harm a body?
And well you know it isn' the dhrink I regard—
Well you know that—but still a body's hardly prepar'd
To pass the only public-house on the road, drivin' home on
    your weddin' night—
It isn' right,
Nor correck, nor friendly, nor in any surt of a concatenation
Lek accordin' to your station—
And disappintin' people that way, when they're trustin'
Your proper feelin's, is quite disgustin'.

    "So I lays my hand on his arm, just by way of signifyin'—
Nothin' more—and behould ye! he cocks hisself up as stiff
    and as dignifyin',
And rip! and rup! and chip! and chup!
And 'There's nobody up,' he says. Nobody up?

And glasses jinglin', and windows blazin',
And people comin'out, and shoutin'amazin'
To stop! But no! but sticks his elbers like skewers in a
     body—
'What!' I says,' not a glass of toddy?
Just for neighbourly dacency!'
'It's surprisin' how early they're goin' to bed,' says he.
'Goin'to bed!' says I. 'Yes,' he says—middlin' snarly—
'Kinvigs's was allis early,' he says, 'partic'lar early'—
And his ould hoss gallopin', and heisin' his hind-quarters, and
     workin'
Like a see-saw, and bumpin' and jerkin',
And sent me flyin', with my head in the bottom of the cart,
     and my feet in the air,
And the rest of me—anywhere.

    "So he puts out his hand—
'Bless my sowl!' he says, 'I thought it was gone!'
'What!' says I. 'The box,' he says, maenin'my box, and
     my weddin' bonnet
Smashed to jammy—'I wish you'd sit upon it,'
He says—the box, of coorse! So I thought I'd be a little
     lovin'
And that—and I comes up lek gradjal, lek shiftin' and shovin'
Lek agen him in a way. And I says, 'I'd like to be with
     you,' says I,
'My own husband,' I says; for I thought it better to try
Was there just a taste
Of anything of a husband in him. So he put his arm around
     my waist—
Not round either—for he couldn'do that—
Not for the stout I am, bein'allis a gintale figger, but just
     like a lath—
Flat
Agen the back o'my stays, and not the smallest curl

Or squeeze in the ould pump-handle, not the smallest in the
    worl'—
And his eyes on the box—and 'There it's goin'!'
He says, and waein'and woin'—
And as restless! And then we got on the mountain; and the
    ling
Was smellin' very sweet in the dark, and a stream began
    ting-ting-ting
Down the other way—very pleasant, and it got couldher,
And I thought it was only a 'spectable thing to put my head
    on his shouldher.

"O dear! he got as crabbit
As an ould buck rabbit;
And he hitched and he hunched, and he cribbed and he
    crunched,
Till he was all bunched
In a lump; and anyway his blades that sharp
And snaggy you might as well ha'leaned your head on the
    backbone of a carp.

"So I didn'care, and I sat up as straight
And as indepandin'. It was gettin' late
When we come to his house; and there was a falla theer
    standin'on the look-out
On the very top of the midden, and jumps down, and grips
    the hoss, and gives a big shout,
And 'Look here!' he says, 'who's goin' to pay me? 'Pay!'
Thinks I—and this ould fool goin' seerchin' away
In all his pockets—and gev a start,
And 'Bless my heart!'
He says, 'hev I lost it? hev I lost it?' and twisses and
    wriggles
Hisself into knots—and the other chap stands and sniggles—
A young chap—And 'Dear me!' says Dan, 'it must ha'
    dropt out on the road comin'—

It's very disthressin',' he says. 'Faith then! you're a rummin,
Says the chap, and like to buss —
'What's the use o'talkin'?' says Dan Cowle, 'I've lost my
    puss.
Where's your puss, Peggy! maybe,' he says, 'you'll not
    mind
Payin' the man,' he says—'if you'll be so kind,'
He says—but oh! that creepin', and that sneakin', and that
    slewin', and that screwin',
Like a conger just. And 'What's a doin'?'
Says I; 'isn' it your own cart you got?'
'Well——no——it's not,'
He says, 'I must confess—
The fact of the matter is,' he says,
'My own cart is bruk very bad,
And I borrowed this one for the occasion.' So I paid the lad.

" 'Aye, aye! his cart is bruk very bad,' says the chap,
'Likewise his trap,
And the phaeton, and the barooch, and the jantin'-car, and
    the family coach-and-four'—
And he gev a roor
Out of hisself, this young divil—
And 'Hurrah for the weddiners!' he says. 'Be civil! be
    civil!'
Says Dan, 'be civil, young man, it would well become ye'—
But says I—'Take your money and your cart,' I says, 'and
    be off with ye, ye scum ye!
Be off!' I says, 'stir your stumps!'
(These Foxdale lumps
Is pirriful.) And Dan with the box on the street, and pokin'
The key in the door—and, you know, I seen the chimbley
    wasn'smokin',
Nor nothin'—nor no cowhouse about that I could see,
Nor no garden, nor a bush, let alone a tree—
But just a crock

Standin' on a rock,
And water runnin' in it very free
At the gable, and slishin' and slushin', and muckin' the street
Under one's feet.

    "And this is the man that tould me he'd make me
So comfible!
But still
You'll not mistake me,
You know me, Misthriss, don't ye! and you know I wouldn'
      flinch,
No, not even if I was deceived—no, not an inch!
On I'd go, through the smooth and the rough,
Content enough—
For richer for poorer, for better for wuss—
Lost his puss!
Had he? lost two! lost twenty!
Give me a man with a lovin' heart, Misthriss, with a lovin'
      heart—
That's plenty—
Plenty for me—navar mind the cart—
With a lovin' heart, and some wit about him—
And I'd navar doubt him,
Misthriss—no! *For better for wuss*—
Them's the words, and didn' the Pazon say them? And I'd
      nuss
His childher, and I'd work, and I'd slave, and I'd die
Before I'd be beat—and still a lie
Is a dirty thing—fore or aft,
As the sailors is sayin'—
But listen again—
Misthriss! Misthriss! you don't know half.

    "So we got in, however, and he groped about, and he
      found a flint-and-steel,
And he skinned his ould knuckles all like a priddha peel,

Streck-streckin' away; and, when he gor a light at last,
You navar seen such a rookery. A dresser there was—
Yis—but hardly a plate or a bason, or any other surt o'
    war',
And a hape of mouldy turmits in a corner there—could,
    comfortless things they are—
And a rot-hole, or a shot-hole, I don't know which, and I
    don't care etha',
And a barrel that looked like male, with a flag or a slate on
    the top of it, and a medha,
And a pot, and nothin' in it, and no fire, if there had been,
    and as for bed or beddin'—
Well, I dedn'throuble, no, faith, I dedn'.

    "It was a house that if you were inside you'd see about
      as much sky as roof,
A surt o' mixthar o' the two, and a touch of harry-long-legses
    and spiders—aw, it's the troof! it's the troof,
The troof I'm tellin'! And the scraas hangin' in rags and
    strings of dirt as black
You couldn' tell were they scraas, or strips tore from a rotten
    ould sack,
Or nettin'or somethin'. And I can tell ye the chap begun,
    as a body might say,
To look rather ashamed of hisself—I think so—in a way—
Yis—he didn'look at me for a bit at all,
But cocked his face agen the wall.

    "And—'It's too late,' he says, 'it's too late for supper, I
      suppose'—
And ye might have sniffed and sniffed till ye straint your nose
Afore you'd ha' got a smell of supper in yandhar place—
But he turned at last, and I saw his face—
Workin', workin', workin'most terrible,
And screwin' the eye, and workin'still—
And—'Let's sit down a bit,' he says, and he studdied the

candle, if ye plaze, and he looks up as innocent as a
    linnet,
And he says, 'That's a nice puss you've got,' he says;' how
    much is there in it?'
And I tould him £4:16s. and 2°d. farlin'—
So he says, 'That's a nice little bit o'money, my darlin'—
Let's see it,' he says.
                  So I gev it to him, ye know;
And he counted it out, I tell ye, every coin of it, very slow—
Very slow he counted—and then—what d'ye think?
Whips it in his pocket! 'A nice lump of jink!'
Says Dan; and he snuggled up closer to me, and he began
    to fiddle and fiddle,
Lek tryin' to span me round the middle—
Some surt o' coortin'? thinks I, *he's improvin', I doubt*—
The ould villyan! He was just tryin' to find out
Had I any more stitched up in my stays!
And a man with such ways—
Would you call him a man! now would ye, Misthriss! would
    ye, though?
That was the fiddlin'—aye! he said it, he said it hisself, the
    ould crow!
Yis, and his dirty ould mouth all of a pucker, and grippin'
    and nippin',
And declarin' he felt the shillin's slippin'
Between the quiltin's—aw dear! aw dear!
But I was enough for him—navar fear!
    "I says—'This is no place for me,' I says; and up I jumps—
'I'm off,' I says; and he rattles his ould stumps—
And—'Off?' he says—'Why you've not opened your box
    yet!'
'Clear out o' the road!' I says. 'I hevn' seen your frocks
    yet,'
He says, 'nor the sheetin' nor nothin'!—just give us that
    key—
It's every bit my proppity!' he says. 'Out o' the way!'

I says, and I gript the box. But if I gript it, he gript it, and
    he shouted and bawled,
And backards and forrards we tugged and we hauled;
And we staggered this way, and we staggered that way,
And higgledy-piggledy, and I cannot tell what way—
But I gev him a run in on the dresser, and his ould back
    bent,
And——down he went!

    "And the crockery—what there was—all smashed—well to
    be sure!
And the turmits rowlin'on the floor—
So the box was mine, and I out on the door.
'Murdher! tieves!' and he run after me full trot—
You're a robber!' he says; 'you've robbed me! everything
    you got
Belongs to me—I'll bring a shuit,' he says; 'I'll bring a
    shuit
For damagers!' he says—the ould brute—
'I'll have your life!' he says,
'Ar'n' you my wife?' he says—
'Murdher!' he says,' 'murdher!'—*Murdher*— your granny,'
I says—'Good-bye, Dan Cowle! good-bye, Danny!'
And I left him standin' in the road; and here I am, as you
    see—
And, Misthriss! no more weddin's, aw good sakes! no, no
    more weddin's for me!"

29

IN THE COACH

Some of the stories which Brown wanted to tell us are very funny and some are very sad but the word-pictures he paints are so vivid that it is easy for us to imagine what the people of that time looked like and how some of the Manx characters behaved. The next four poems are spoken by various passengers in a horse-drawn stage coach, probably going from Castletown to Douglas. You can read more stories from In the Coach *in* The Collected Poems of T. E. Brown.

CONJERGAL RIGHTS

This means "conjugal" rights; the legal rights husbands and wives gain over each other when they marry. At the time of the poem, the rights were mainly in the husband's favour and chief amongst these was his right to all the property the wife owned when she married or which she gained later.

About the only conjugal right a woman gained on marriage was the right to her husband's affection. Unmarried women had the right to own properety but there were always mean or greedy men around who married women just to get their hands on money, land or a house. This story is told by one such greedy man whose bride, on her wedding day, suddenly realises that he is more interested in the house which she owns than he is in her.

Words: jink of her=look of her; **tight**=drunk; **grayshurs**=gracious; **farlin'**=farthing (a quarter of an old penny); **guy heng**=go hang; **kilt**=killed; **a jilt**=jilted; **chaber**=cheaper; **sthraw**=straw spread on floor of the coach as matting; **ordashurs**=audacious; **no suttlement goin'- amakin'**=no marriage settlement to be made; **massy**=mercy; **my chree**=my heart (my dear); **girnin'**=grinning; **imprince**=impudence; **aburt**=about; **yandhar**=yonder (that particular thing); **ither**=either; **lar't**=let it.

See also: Peggy's Wedding (p.20), The Pazons (p.35).

CONJERGAL RIGHTS

Conjergal rights! conjergal rights!
I don't care for the jink of her and I don't care for the jaw
      of her,
But I'll have the law of her.
Conjergal rights! yis, yis, I know what I'm sayin'
Fuss-rate, Misthress Corkhill, fuss-rate, Misther Cain,
And all the people in the coach—is there a man or a woman
      of the lot of ye—
Well now, that's what I wudn' have thought of ye,
I wudn' raelly—No, I *haven' got a little sup,*
Not me—is there one of ye that wudn' stand up
For conjergal rights?
No, ma'am, tight's
Not the word, not a drop since yesterday. But lizzen, good
      people, lizzen!
I'll have her in the coorts, I'll have her in prison—
It's the most scandalous thing you ever—What! this woman
      and her daughter—
It's clane murder, it's abslit manslaughter,
Aye, and I wudn' trus' but beggamy, that's what it is—
      Married yesterday mornin'
In Kirk Breddhan Church, and not the smallest taste of
      warnin',
Takes her to her house in Castletown,
And jus' for I axed a quashtin—and I'll be boun'
It's a quashtin any one of you wud have axed—picks a quarrel,
      makes a row,
The two of them, aye, the two of them—bow-wow!
Hammer and tungs! sends for a pleeceman, puts me to the
      door—
But I'll owe her! I'll owe her!
Aisy, Mr. Cretney? No, I'll not be aisy;
It's enough to make a body crazy,
That's what it is, and the supper on the table,

And the hoss in the stable.
And I said nothin', nor I done nothin'. Aw, if there's law in
        the land,
Law or justice, I'll have it, d'ye understand?
Do ye see the thing? My grayshurs! married is married,
Isn' it? what? and me that carried
The woman's box. And that isn' all; what raison? what
        sense?
Think of the expense! think of the expense!
Don't ye know? God bless me! The certif'cake, that's
        hafe-a-crown,
And the licence, that's five shillin', money down, money down!
And not a farlin' off for cash, these Pazons, not a farlin';
And said she was my darlin'
And all to that, guy heng! it's thrue! it's thrue!
And look at me now! boo-hoo-oo-oo!
Yis, cryin' I am, and no wondher—
You don't see me it's that dark in the coach. By the livin'
        thundher
I'm kilt mos'ly, that's what I am, almos' kilt
With throuble and disthress and all. *A jilt,*
You say, *a jilt?* But married, married, married, d'ye hear?
Married, Misthress Creer,
Married afore twelve at Kirk Breddhan,
Married, a reg'lar proper weddin'
And no mistake,
And this woman . . . O my gough! don't spake of her!
        don't spake!
It's me that's spakin'? Yis, and I will! I will!
Who's to spake if I amn'? But still—
It's lek you don't see, the coach is so dark, and no light
        from these houses,
But feel of this new coat, and the pair of new trousis,
Bought o' puppose, o' puppose! what else?
Bran new; and the shirt and the frells,
And the cuffs and the collar, every d— thing
As bran and as new as a gull's wing—

And all to plaze her, and to look accordin'
To the occasion, and to do her credit, and ho'rdin'
The teens of months. And O, if I'd only borrowed
        them from a neighbour!
That's the thing, but bought them, bought them! and even
        so they might ha' been chaber,
Yis, they might, at another shop. But you don' see the way
        I'm goin',
No, no, you don'—
But I'd lek you to—the tears! I'm jus' slushin' the sthraw
With the tears, makin' the coach all damp for the people—
        yis, I know I am, but I'll have the law, I'll have the law.
Just a quashtin about a bit of proppity,
The house, in fac', the very house we come into, d'ye see?
The house, her house! Of coorse! of coorse! But
        good-ness grayshurs!
Who doesn' know the law about a thing like that? the iggorant!
        the ordashurs!
If ever there was a thing on God's earth
That was mine, it was yandhar house! But it isn' worth
Talkin'-no! There's people that'll go against anything.
        But what! no suttlement goin' a-makin',
Nor nothin', jus' everything goin' a-takin'
Undher the common law of matrimony theer—
At my massy! at my massy! With your lave, Mr. Tear,
At my massy, sir. You'll 'scuse me.
But you know the law. Married—my chree! my chree!
What iss "married," if that isn'? it's as plain as a dus'bin—
Your own dear lovin' husbin'
As kind as kind!
See the beauty of it! And "all that's thine is mine,"
Isn' it sayin' that in the Bible?
And surely the woman is li'ble
As well as the man; and to "love, honour, and obey,"
Isn' that what they say?
But it's my heart, that's it! my poor broken heart! aw dear!
        aw dear!

And my feelin's! my feelin's! and that son of mine girnin'
      from ear to ear,
And his lip, and his imprince, and his disrespeck,
And the waste and the neglec'—
O, it's awful! it's awful! O, the wounds that there's no
      healin's!
O, my feelin's! my feelin's!
But I'll see aburt, I will, I'll see aburt—
The dirt!
The wife of my bosom! Don't be mockin'!
I heard a woman laughing: its shockin'
That a woman'd laugh at the lek of such doin's, yis, it is,
Downright wickedness—
A woman that I could name—
Fie for shame! fie for shame!
But I'll have law. Look here! Is James Gell a lawyer? You'll
      hardly uphould me
He isn', will ye? James Gell—the Attorney-Gineral: well,
      that's the man that tould me.
Did I spake to him about it? was I axin' him afore
I was anything to her?
Sartinly! my gough! was I goin' to run my neck into a noose,
And navar no 'pinion nor...I'm not such a goose
As yandhar ither, I've gorrit in writin', yis, I have,
I've gorrit here-aw, you'll get lave! you'll get lave!
Not aisy to read, but God bless me! where's my specs?
      But lar't! lar't!
It's my feelin's: O, my heart! my heart!
My poor heart! my poor heart! boo-hoo-oo-oo! Aye, and
      you'd think there'd be
Some semperthy,
Some...Crow, open this door and let me out! there's no
      regard with ye
For a man's...I'll not ride another yard with ye...
Theer then! theer! No, I'll have none of your good-nights...
Conjergal rights! conjergal rights!

THE PAZONS

T. E. Brown was a parson's son and an ordained clergyman himself so he understood the church and its ministers. He also had a tremendous love for his fellow man and understood their temptations, their predudices and their double standards very well.

In this amusing poem, the speaker is a hypocritical fellow, very like the man portrayed in Conjergal Rights. He says one thing behind a person's back and the opposite to their face but Brown here reveals his tolerance of this human weakness. Perhaps Brown was remembering his father's attitude, for he once wrote, "My father would have considered he was 'taking a liberty' if he had confronted the sinner with his sin. .... But don't suppose ... that the 'weak bretheren' thought he was conniving at their weakness. Not they: they saw the delicacy of his conduct"

Like many "Barrack-Room-Lawyers", though, the character in this poem has an ability to make the truth look slightly ridiculous at times but fine word pictures are presented of, for instance, the part-time preacher wrestling with his own mind to find the words to give the strength of his own religious beliefs to his listeners.

Words: **pazons**=parsons (Church of England clergymen); **despard**=desperate; **rubbage**=rubbish; **tithe**=one tenth of a person's income taken by law since Old Testament times for the Church; **glebe**=small piece of agricultural land belonging to the Church and used for the benefit of the clergyman; **fuss**=first; **bates**=beats; **pulfit**=the pulpit in a church or chapel from which sermons are preached; **steer**=stairs (of the pulpit); **a local**=an unordained Local Preacher on the local "plan" (time table) of the Methodist church; **collec'**=collect (equal stress on both syllables), one of many set prayers recited at specified times in the Church of England services; **pestlin'**=pounding or beating the pulpit for added emphasis; **rant**=members of the "Primitive" branch of the Methodist Church were nick-named "The Ranters", so here the word is taken as an insult; **farlin rush**=rush light (costing a farthing) in the pulpit to illuminate the preacher's notes; **thallure** (dy liooar)=galore or enough; **laste**=least; **idikkilis**=ridiculous; **popery**=to do with Roman Catholicism and the Pope; **burn**=burn in the everlasting fire of Hell.

THE PAZONS

What's the gud of these Pazons? They're the most despard
     rubbage go'n',
Reg'lar humbugs they are. Show me a Pazon, show me a
     drone!
Livin' on the fat of the land, livin' on the people's money
The same's the drones is livin' on the beeses honey.
Aw bless ye! the use of them? not the smallest taste in the
     world, no!

Grindin' down the honest workin' man, just so;
Suckin' the blood of the poor and needy,
And as greedy's greedy.
See the tithes, see the fees, see the glebes and all;
What's the call
For the lek? and their wives go'n' a takin' for ladies, and
        their childhar go'n' sendin' to College
Like the fuss of the land. Aw, it bates all knowledge
The uprisement of the lek! And fingerin' with their piannas,
Them that shud be singin' their hosannahs
To the King of glory constant. Clap them in the pulfit theer,
What can they do! Aw, come down the steer! come down
        the steer,
And don't be disgracin' yourself that way! That's what I've
        been thinkin' many a time—
And let a praecher take his turn, a local, aye, just try'm!
Aw, give your people a chance to get salvation.
"Blow ye the trumpet in Zion!" That's the style, and the
        prespiration
Pourin' out all over his body! See the wrestlin',
And the poor Pazon with his collec' and his pestlin'
And his gosp'lin'. *Gospel!* Let it sound abroad,
The rael gospel of God!
Aw then the happy I am!
Give us the Lamb! give us the Lamb!
But he can't, I tell ye, he can't—
What's that young man sayin' theer—rant?
Rant indeed, is that what he's learnin'
At Oxfoot College, to revile the spirit that's burnin'
In the hearts of the faithful? Aye, and let it burn, let it blaze!
But here's the Pazon, if ye plaze,
Cocked up with his little twinkle of a farlin' rush,
And'll hauk and blush,
And his snips and his snaps
And his scrips and his scraps,
And endin' up with the Lord's Prayer quite sudden
Lek the ould woman's sauce to give a notion of a puddin',...

Aye, puddin', and drabbin' with their swishups and dishups
Of the stale ould broth of the law! If all the hands of all
      the bishops
Was goin' crookin' over his head, he wudn' be a praecher,
Not him, *nor* a taecher.
You can't be married without a Pazon? Can't I though?
Can't I, Masther Crow?
Give me the chance: I'm a married man with a fam'ly comin',
But if it plazed the Lord to take Mrs. Creer, d'ye think there's
      a woman
'd refuse to go with me before the High Bailiff down
At Castletown,
And ger' a slick of matrimony put upon us?
Honest?
Yes, honest thallure: *but holy, "holy matrimony," they're*
sayin'—
Holy your grandmother!—At laste, I mane,
And astin' your pardon, Mrs. Clague!
But the idikkilis people is about the lek o' yandhar—Aisy with
      your leg,
Masthar Callow; thank ye! that'll do—
Yis, Mrs. Clague, and crizzenin's and funarls too—
Shuperstition, just shuperstition, the whole kit,
Most horrid, just popery, clane popery, that's it—
Aye, popery and schamin' and a lie and a delusion and snares
To get money out of the people, which is the Lord's and
      not theirs!
Money, money every turn,
Money, money—pay or burn!
And where does it come from? I said it before, and I say
      it again,
Out of the sweat of the workin' man,
Aw these priests! these priests! these priests—
Down with them, I say. The brute beasts
Has more sense till us, that's willin' to pay blackmail
To a set of rascals, to a pack of——Good evenin', Pazon
      Gale!

Good evenin', sir, good evenin'! Step up, sir! Make room,
Make room for our respected Vicar—And may I persume
To ax how is Mrs. Gale, sir, and the family?
Does this weather agree—
Rather damp, I dessay! And the Governor's got knighted?
I'm delighted to see you, sir, delighted, delighted!

In the times when these poems were written, dozens of Manx boats and hundreds of Manx seamen journeyed all over the World. This poem is spoken by a simple (some might say, silly) young woman who is wild with excitement as, in Part A., she goes to meet her husband, Billy, whom she hasn't seen for a year and, in Part B., she shows him off to the passengers as he joins the party in the coach.

Words: **ducks**=smart trousers made of untwilled linen or cotton; **millish ven=**sweet woman; **chiss**=seaman's chest for his belongings; **Crid shen?** (C'rid shen)=What is that?
See also: Mater Dolorossa (p.112); The Christening (p.15).

GOING TO MEET HIM

A. Yes, yes, I'll be seein' him, seein' Billy
This very night—aw, I'm almost silly
With the thought. Yes, Mrs. Quayle, just a year away,
And he's comin' home this very day.
Billy! Billy! aw, the foolish I am!
And you'll 'scuse me, ladies, won't ye now? Aw, I'll be as qui't as a lamb,
Yes, I will: and it isn' right
To be carryin' on like this afore people, but aw, the delight!
O! I wonder how he'll be lookin'; he's that handsome and gud,
Aw yes, aw dear! I wud, I wud,
I wud fly, I wud die! O the darling! O! it's shockin',
And I can't keep qui't, no, I can't, no, I can't, and it's no use o' talkin'.
But I'll try, Mrs. Quayle, you know me; yes, I'll try, I'll do my best,
O! I will though, and only proper lek. But how'l he be drest?
O Billy, Billy! will he have his white ducks? ho, ho!
It's me that 'd make them like the driven snow;
But these Liverpool washerwomen—chut! the nasty things! aw, I'll be bail
No notion whatever, no, they haven'; what did ye say, Mrs. Quayle?
Not to be expctin' too much and I'll not be disappointed? and *I'd batthar—*
What, Mrs. Quayle, *batthar* what, what? what? I've got the latthar!
He's comin'! he's comin'! "On the spree?" did ye say?

Like the way
With such, Mrs. Quayle? With such!
Mrs. Quayle! Mrs. Quayle! Who then? whuch?
This coach is chokin' me, give me air—
No, no! it isn' fair,
Navar! no, navar! navar!
No, no! you're clavar,
You've seen a dale,
Mrs. Quayle,
A dale, no doubt, but that you'll navar see,
For I love Billy, and Billy loves me!
Is that plain? don't you know that? It cudn'! it cudn'!
But ye come upon me that sudden.
No, no! that's not Billy, nor natur', nor nothin'; that's foolishness—
But I can't rest—
This coach is close—the hot I am and the coul'!
(Chorus of conscious women) "Poor sowl! poor sowl!"

B. Now then, now then, what do you say now?
Here he is, and I think you'll allow,
Eh, Mrs. Quayle, you'll allow, I think,
Not the smallest sign of drink.
And I ast your pardon humble I do—
I'm forgettin' myself. But is it you?
Is it you? is it you? Whisper then,
The *millish ven!*
Close, Billy, close—
God knows
I love you, Billy, and you love me,
Don't you, Billy? my chree! my chree!
Aw, just to hear—
Chut! I'm foolish, but O, the dear!
The—*Steady*, did ye say? yis, Billy, yis!
Steady it is.
Now, Mrs. Quayle, is he drunk or sober?
Poor ould Billy! And last October

He sailed, poor chap! And *it's me that's drunk*—
With joy you mane? And have you got your trunk—
What am I talkin'? your chiss—dear me! and didn' I see't
Comin' along the street—
Of coorse, and mended—
You tould me. O! isn' all this beautiful? isn' it splendid?
Closer, Billy, closer then!
Crid shen?
Nothin', but . . . lizzen, Billy, whisp'rin's free
I love Billy, and he loves me . . .
Do you, Billy? as God's above,
Do you love
Me, Billy? The word, Billy, as soft as soft—
What am I thinkin' of?
Aw, ye said it, ye said it. And now I'll trouble ye
Is he drunk or sober, this young man, W.
Sayle, by name? Aw, you'll 'scuse me, won't ye?
Aw I didn' mane to 'front ye,
Aw nothin' of the surt! Only, ye see, the glad
I am it's fit to drive me mad.
And I'm rather young . . . at laste, not that oul',
You'll 'scuse me, won't ye . . .
(Chorus of conscious women) " Poor sowl! poor sowl!"

41

JUS' THE SHY

Manx people have always thought of themselves as being shy and not "pushy", particularly in the presence of strangers. This poem is set in the days when Manx boats fished all round Britain's coasts and tells the story of a fleet of twenty vessels returning from the North Sea. Whilst sheltering in a Scottish loch, all the crews are invited to dinner at a big castle but the men are all too shy to go.

In all the "dialect" poems, Brown uses interesting spellings to let you know how some people spoke in those times. You also need to know that a Mhellia is the Manx celebration at harvest time; in the poem Brown spells it as "melya" - which is the correct way to pronounce it.

Words: mayve=maybe (in Gaelic, "b" and "v" frequently interchange); **comfible**=comfortable; **burgee**=owner's or company's small swallow-tailed flag on a vessel, but here used jokingly for a house-flag; **Fargher**=pronounced Faragher; **heisin**=hoisting; **.... and the curks drawin**=lots of corks were being drawn out of wine bottles in preparation for the feast; **star'**=stare; **bitendin**=pretending; **lek**=like or likely; **chiarn** (Gaelg)=Lord; **bogh**=a clumsy simpleton; **lavin**=leaving.

JUS' THE SHY

YES, comin' home from the North Sea fishin' we were, past
      John o' Grotes,
Past the Pentlands and Cape Wrath theer, twenty boats
There'd be of us, and eight men and boys to every one, and
      how many are you making that?
A hundred-and-sixty, "says you—You're smart though, what?
And sure enough it is—aw this ciphrin' and figgurin' and
      recknin', aw grand! grand!
Well, when we hauled to the southward, the wind turned a
      foul, you'll understand;
So we made for a bay though, the lot of us; ter'ble narra it
      was to get in—
That bay—but spreadin' out astonhin',
And the room you navar seen—acres! acres! So swings to
      an anchor for all
As aisy as aisy, and plenty to spare, just that we could call
The time o' day and that: it's comfible, you know, like
      yandhar, and mayve a matthar
Of ten fathom—good houldin', fuss-rate ridin', couldn' be
      batthar.

42

And at the top of the bay there was a castle, ter'ble though,
Aw, bless ye, ter'ble uncommon, and the gardens theer all in
      a row,
And all above one another; and some guns that was took
      from the Rooshians, and a tower, and a flag goin'
      a-haulin'—
I don' know the burgee, but as broad as a good tarpaulin;
And over the door, cut to a dot, aw, open your eyes the
      widest you can!
Over the door, if you plaze, over the door, what next? God
      bless us! the three legs of Man!
That was the thing. My gough! the wondher we had;
And this and that; but at last Billy Fargher said
It muss ha' been some of these ould Earls or Dukes, or their
      daughters, or their nieces, or their cousins
(Of coorse, there'd be dozens)
That got married on yandhar lek—
At laste you'd expeck
There'd be some workin' in and out; and blood is blood,
That's aisy understood;
And navar ashamed of the ould flag, not her; but heisin' it
      to the wind, and carvin' it on the stone, like defyin',
Lek as bould as a lion.
Now there was a ter'ble great lady livin' in this Castle, mind!
Aye, a lady, bless ye! and no mitake, grand, no doubt, but
      kind.
And she come to see us, aye, and she said she was once on
      the Islan',
And the people was that good to her, and that civil, and that
      smilin',
And that plazzant, she said, *that she couldn' forget it,* she said,
No, she said; *and it wasn' no use,* she said,
They were nice people, she said, *the nice you couldn' tell;*
That's what she said and she liked them well.
And she wouldn' take no res' of us but we muss promise
      then and theer
To have dinner with her, aye! dinner, think of that now! a

hundred-and-sixty of us—what? aw, I'll sweer.
Dinner though; so promised sure enough; and the day come,
And there wasn' a sowl of us went, not a sowl, by gum!
No! and the pipers blawin,
And the curks drawin,
And the preparation they'd be havin', so I'm toul',
And there wasn' a sowl, no, not a sowl.
And what for was that? What for? Just the shy, the shy,
That's the what for, and that's the why,
And that's the way with the Manx; aw, it is though, aw,
      they are, they are,
Mos' despard shy: aw, it's a pity for all but star'
They will, and wink and nudge and poke one another—
"Are you goin', and you?" and takin' rises, and all to that,
Till you can't tell is it your granny's cat
Or what is it that's doin' on you, but you feel jus' a reg'lar fool
And all the time bitendin' to be as cool as cool.
Aw dear! it's a pity! a pity! aw, a rum lot!
But, whether or not,
The great lady was agate of us again,
'Deed for sure she was, and she seen the men
Was shy of the dinner; but it's lek she thought
It was on account of not knowin' how to behave theerselves
      the way they ought
With theer knives and theer plates and the lek; so axed
      them to tay—
Aw, she muss ha' been a kind lady anyway!
And we promised faithful, and the day come, and she sent
      and she sent
And there wasn' a one of us went.
The shy, did ye say? Sartinly, nothin but the shy,
That's the way we are; aye,
Treminjus though. I was raelly sorry for her, I was, I tell
      ye,
And all the throuble that was at her theer, fit for a melya,
And the dappointed—what? and, altogather, my chiarn!
These Manx chaps isn' fit, no they ar'n'—

Ter'ble boghs!
     Well the wind veered round, and we all sailed for the
      southward,
Excep' two boats. Now, d'ye think she'd ha' bothered
About such dunkies? Well, that's jus' what she did,
Perseverin', aye! and considherin', and waitin'. Turn your
     quid!"
Says Juan Jem, lek futhee, lek *no hurry!* you know
Lek *aisy* all! lek *keep her so!*
Lek wait and see! Patient, is it? But anyway the strong
The kindness was in her—that's it, and the long-
Suff'rin' lek, and navar not no capers of takin' offince.
My gough! it's many a time I've thought of it since.
What did she do but down to these chaps that was lavin'
     behind—
Sixteen of them, aye—and axed them theer as kind as kind—
To tay? most sartin; what else? and I tell ye they took heart
     and went,
And enjoyed theerselves to the full the same's it might be
     you or any other gent.
But the res'? you're wond'rin'. Chut!
Jus' the shy, and nothin' *but*
The shy. Aw, no use a' talkin',
The shy it's shawkin'.
No raison, says you; not a bit.
Amazin', says you. Well, that's all you'll get,
That the raison, and the for and the why—
Jus' the shy!

THE FO'C'S'LE YARNS

These stories are long and, to make them interesting, Brown has a sailor called Tom Baynes tell them to his shipmates in the cramped crew's quarters in the bow of a sailing ship. This part of a vessel is known as the "fo'c's'le" (folk'sul) which is a shortened version of "forecastle". Tom Baynes is a rough, boastful but soft-hearted man and it is said that T. E. Brown had an old salt called Bob Lucas from Peel in mind when he created the character. Had he not been a university educated scholar, Brown would probably have wanted to be a seafarer and he once wrote, "Tom Baynes simply is I".

BETSY LEE

The first of the Fo'c's'le Yarns is Betsy Lee *and some excerpts begin overleaf. It tells how, when Tom was growing up in a little cottage by the seashore, he fell in love with the girl next door. Her name was Betsy Lee. When Tom and Betsy are in their 'teens the Lee family moves to a farm about a mile away but Tom visits Betsy every day and helps her to milk the cows. But a lawyer's clerk called Richard Taylor has also fallen in love with Betsy and the jealousy between the two young men causes both to behave very badly towards each other and the heartbreak caused by this rivalry eventually causes Betsy's death, though the poem does have a peaceful ending. On the next few pages we have printed short extracts from the poem but we hope that sometime you will read the complete version from another book.*

YOUNG LIFE AND YOUNG LOVE
(From Betsy Lee)

Words: courtin (coo'ur'tin)=courting;   **hisn**=the absolute (rather than adjectival) form of "his"; **clap of shoot**=fall of soot down a chimney;   **risin**=rising;   **pisin** (**pie'zin**)=poison;   **lumps**=good-sized lads;   **marks**=cross-bearings taken at sea of features on land; these position the boats over the best places for fishing;   **signs**=signs of wind, weather and sea conditions affecting the chances of catching fish;   **lines**=long-lines: fishing lines with up to two hundred hooks attached along their length. These had a heavy weight on the bottom and a large float on the surface and were left in the sea for hours at a time;   **cobblin'**=cobbling: pulling the boat safely up onto the cobbles out of the reach of the tide;   **yawl**=any sort of small, open fishing boat and not necessarily one having a yawl rig;   **dramin'**=dreaming;   **creels**=lobster or crab pots;   **gut**=possibly refers to the catgut joining hooks to the fishing line but could mean the fish guts used as bait; **slut**=a lively slip of a girl: (not a term of abuse);   **coil**=clutter, rattle, business of living; **furder**=further;   **wuss**=worse;   **gray ribs**=the hard undulations formed where freshwater flows down a beach to the sea;   **bumbees**=bumble bees;   **goss**=gorse;   **peltin'**=pelting -

throwing stones at; **gibbins**=sand-eels; **wench**=lass; **sickle**=a gibbin sickle for flicking eels out of the sand; **one for his knob**=originally this meant an extra one of things being counted, such as an extra herring or an extra loaf of bread for good measure, but children extended its use to mean a punch to the head; **brew=**broogh, grassy bank; **mawther**=mother; **yandhar=**yonder; **mailie**=cow without horns; **brat**=apron; **buzz of a reel**=the fast buzz of a fishing reel as the weighted line is let out; **skute**=squirt (but isn't this a much better word?); **kermoonicate**=communicate; **ransy-tansy-tissimitee**=chorus of an old children's dancing-song.

YOUNG LIFE AND YOUNG LOVE
(From Betsy Lee)

Now most of you lads has had a spell
Of courtin' and that, and it's hard to tell
How ever a youngster comes to fancy
That of all the gels it's Jinny or Nancy,
Or Mary or Betsy that must be hisn.
I don't know how it is or it isn',
But some time or other it comes to us all
Just like a clap of shoot or a squall,
Or a snake or a viper, or some such dirt,
Creep—creep—creepin' under your shirt,
And slidin' and slippin' right into your breast,
And makin' you as you can't get rest:
And it works and it works till you feel your heart risin'—
God knows what it is if it isn' pisin.

You see—we're a roughish set of chaps,
That's brought up rough on our mammies' laps;
And we grow, and we run about shoutin' and foolin'
Till we gets to be lumps and fit for the schoolin'.
Then we gets to know the marks and the signs,
And we leaves the school, and we sticks to the lines,
Baitin' and settin' and haulin' and that,
Till we know every fish from a whale to a sprat.
And we gets big and strong, for it do make you stronger

To row a big boat, and to pull at a conger.
Then what with a cobblin' up of the yawl,
And a patchin' and mendin' the nets for the trawl,
And a risin' early and a goin' to bed late,
And a dramin' of scollops as big as a plate,
And the hooks and the creels and the oars and the gut,
You'd say there's no room for a little slut.
But howsomdever it's not the case,
And a pretty face is a pretty face;
And through the whole coil, as bright as a star,
A gel slips in, and there you are!

　　　Well, that was just the way with me
And the gel I'm speakin' of—Betsy Lee.
Ah, mates! it's wonderful too—the years
You may live dead-on-end with your eyes and your ears
Right alongside of the lass that's goin'
To be your sweetheart, and you never knowin'!

　　　That's the way. For her father and mine
Was neighbours, and both in the fisherman line;
And their cottages stood on the open beach,
With a nice bit of garden aback of them each.
You know the way them houses is fixed,
With the pigs and the hens and the childher mixed;
And the mothers go round when the nights begin,
And whips up their own, and takes them in.
Her father was terrible fond of flowers,
And his garden was twice as handsome as ours—
A mortal keen eye he had for the varmin,
And his talk was always of plantin' and farmin'.
He had roses hangin' above his door,
Uncommon fine roses they was to be sure,
And the joy of my heart was to pull them there,
And break them in pieces on Betsy's hair.
Not that Betsy was much of a size

At the time I mean, but she had big eyes,
So big and so blue and so far asunder,
And she looked so sollum I used to wonder.
That was all—just baby play,
Knockin' about the boats all day,
And sometimes a lot of us takin' hands
And racin' like mad things over the sands.
Ah! it wouldn' be bad for some of us
If we'd never gone furder, and never fared wuss;
If we'd never grown up, and never got big,
If we'd never took the brandy swig,
If we were skippin' and scamp'rin' and cap'rin' still
On the sand that lies below the hill,
Crunchin' its gray ribs with the beat
Of our little patterin' naked feet
If we'd just kept childher upon the shore
For ever and ever and ever more!

     Now the beauty of the thing when childher plays is
The terrible wonderful length the days is.
Up you jumps, and out in the sun,
And you fancy the day will never be done;
And you're chasin' the bumbees hummin' so cross
In the hot sweet air among the goss,
Or gath'rin' bluebells, or lookin' for eggs,
Or peltin' the ducks with their yalla legs,
Or a climbin' and nearly breakin' your skulls,
Or a shoutin' for divilment after the gulls,
Or a thinkin' of nothin', but down at the tide
Singin' out for the happy you feel inside.
That's the way with the kids, you know,
And the years do come and the years do go,
And when you look back it's all like a puff,
Happy and over and short enough.

     Well, I never took notions on Betsy Lee,—
Nor no more did she, I suppose, on me,

Till one day diggin' upon the sand—
Gibbins, of course you'll understand,
A lad that was always a cheeky young sprout,
Began a pullin' of Betsy about;
And he worried the wench till her shoulders were bare,
And he slipped the knot of her beautiful hair,
And down it come, as you may say,
Just like a shower of golden spray,
Blown this way and that by a gamesome breeze,
And a rip-rip-ripplin' down to her knees.
I looked at Betsy—aw dear! how she stood!
A quiv'rin' all over, and her face like blood!
And her eyes, all wet with tears, like fire,
And her breast a swellin' higher and higher!
And she gripped her sickle with a twitchy feel,
And her thumb started out like a coil of steel,
And a cloud seemed to pass from my eyes, and a glory
Like them you'll see painted sometimes in a story,
Breathed out from her skin; and I saw her no more
The child I had always thought her before,
But wrapped in the glory, and wrapped in the hair,
Every inch of a woman stood pantin' there.
So I ups with my fist, as I was bound,
And one for his nob, and knocks him down,
But from that day, by land and sea,
I loved her! O, I loved her! my Betsy Lee.

COWS
(from Betsy Lee)

We have put the next three excerpts together but they come from three separate parts of Betsy Lee. *T. E. Brown not only shows his own love for natural things here but also the affinity that the stockman has with the animals in his care.*

Words: **bas'es**=beasts, cattle; **strooghin'**=stroking, rubbing one leg against another; **drabs**=moistens; **aisy**=easy; **tantaran**=a Manx version of "tarantara" —the sound of the huntsman's horn, here compared with the ringing sound as milk from the cow hits the side of the bucket; **Lawyer gent**=Tom's rival for Betsy's affections; **accumpliment**=accompaniment; **slew**=turn; **agin**=against; **dip**=the pith of a rush dipped in hot wax or animal fat and, when solidified, used as a candle; **yocked**=yoked chain or wooden frame round cow's neck which permits vertical movement but keeps her in the stall; **ghos'es**=ghosts.

COWS
(from Betsy Lee)

I never thought on for the whys or the hows,
But I was always terrible fond of cows.
Now aren't they innocent things—them bas'es?
And havn' they got ould innocent faces?
A strooghin' their legs that lazy way,
Or a standin' as if they meant to pray—
They're that sollum and lovin' and studdy and wise,
And the butter meltin' in their big eyes!
Eh? what do you think about it, John?
Is it the stuff they're feedin' on—
The clover and meadow-grass and rushes,
And them goin' pickin' among the bushes,
And snifffin' the dew when it's fresh and fine,
The sweetest brew of God's own wine!
And the smell of the harbs gets into their sowls,
And works and works, and rowls and rowls,
Till it tightens their tits, and drabs their muzzle—
Well, it's no use o' talkin'—it's a regular puzzle;
But you'll notice the very people that's got to atten'
To the like, is generally very aisy men.

Well, mostly every ev'rin', you see,
I was up at the milkin', with Betsy Lee.
For when she was milkin', she was always singin';
I don't know what was it—maybe the ringin'
Of the milk comin' tearin' into the can,
With a swish and a swelsh and a tantaran,
A makin' what the Lawyer gent
Was callin' a sort of *accumpliment*.
But the look of a cow is enough to do it,
And her breath, and her neck, the way she'll slew it—
As if she was sayin', the patient she stood:—
"Milk away! it's doin' me good."
And the sun goin' down, and the moon comin' up,
And maybe you takin' a little sup,
And the steam of the hay, and your forehead pressin'
Agin her round side! But, for all, it's a blessin'
When they're nice and quiet, for there's some of them rough,
And kicky and pushy and bould enough.

Well, winter come, and then the cows
Was goin' a milkin' in the house.
And if you want peace and quietness,
It's in a cow-house you'll get it the best.
For the place is so warm, and their breath is so sweet,
And the nice straw bedding about their feet,
And hardly any light at all,
But just a dip stuck on to the wall,
And them yocked in the dark as quiet as ghos'es,
And a feelin' for each other's noses.
And, bless me! sometimes you'd hardly be knowin'
It was them, excep' for their chewin' and blowin'.
Aw, many a time I've felt quite queer
To see them standin' so orderly there.
Is it the Lord that makes them so still?
Aw, I like them craythurs terrible!
Aye, aye! the sea for the leks of us!
It's God's own work (though treacherous!);
But for peace and rest and that—d'ye see?
Among the cows is the place for me.

PARSON GALE
(from Betsy Lee)

Rectors or Vicars of parishes are often known by the more intimate title of "parson". Using the word implies some emotion; people might say, "He was a horrid parson", or "a jolly parson" but they would usually say only "the vicar" or "the rector". T. E. Brown knew many clergymen and Pazon Gale is a mixture of the best of them.

Words: **pazon**=parson; **bail**=bold enough to state with confidence; **spakin'** (spay'kin)=speaking; **the take**=what a fisherman receives after the catch is sold and the money shared out between the crew, the owner and the boat; **twis'**=twist: tobacco leaves twisted tightly together like rope; **agate** (a'<u>gate</u>)=with; **mortal**=very (a corruption of "immortal" implying an excess stronger than nature e.g "mortal quick" or "mortal good at ..."); **middlin'**=middle way between, medium; **that's allowed**=that's admitted; **partickler**=particular; **rings on their fingers etc.**=an exaggeration based on the nursery rhyme "Ride a cock-horse to Banbury Cross"; **vice**=voice.

PAZON GALE
(from Betsy Lee)

Now the grandest ould pazon, I'll be bail,
That ever was, was ould Pazon Gale.
Aw, of all the kind and the good and the true!
And the aisy and free, and "How do you do?
And how's your mother, Tom, and the fishin'?"
Spakin' that nice, and allis wishin'
Good luck to the boats, and—"How's the take?"
And blessin' us there for Jesus' sake.
And many a time he'd come out and try
A line, and the keen he was, and the spry!
And he'd sit in the stern, and he'd tuck his tails,
And well he knew how to handle the sails.
And sometimes, if we were smookin', he'd ax
For a pipe, and then we'd be turnin' our backs,
Lettin' on never to see him, and lookin'
This way and that way, and him a smookin',
Twis' as strong and as black as tar,

And terrible sollum and regular.
Bless me! the sperrit that was in him too,
Houldin' on till all was blue!
And only a little man, but staunch,
With a main big heart aback of his paunch!
Just a little round man—but you should ha' seen him agate
Of a good-sized conger or a skate
His arms as stiff, and his eye afire,
And every muscle of him like wire!

      But avast this talk! What! what did you say?
Tell us more about the Pazon—eh?
Well, well! he was a pazon—yis!
But there's odds of pazons, that's the way it is.
For there's pazons now that's mortal proud,
And some middlin' humble, that's allowed.
And there's pazons partikler about their clothes,
And rings on their fingers, and bells on their toes
And there's pazons that doesn' know your names,
"Shut the gate, my man!" and all them games.
And there's pazons *too* free—I've heard one cuss
As hard and as hearty as one of us.
But Pazon Gale—now I'll give you his size,
He was a simple pazon, and lovin' and wise.
That's what he was, and quiet uncommon,
And never said much to man nor woman;
Only the little he said was meat
For a hungry heart, and soft and sweet,
The way he said it: and often talkin'
To hisself, and lookin' down, and walkin'.
Quiet he was, but you couldn' doubt
The Pazon was knowin' what was he about.
Aye, many a time I've seen his face
All slushed with tears, and him tellin' of *grace*
And *mercy* and that, and his vice so low,
But trimblin'—aw, we liked him though!

SAILORS ASHORE

(from Betsy Lee)

After Betsy dies, Tom Baynes loses most of his self-control. He "sails foreign" to earn money which he then spends mainly on drink when he is ashore. In this extract we have a telling vignette of what life was like for such men when they were in England's busy seaports between voyages.

If you have a copy of the whole Betsy Lee poem, you will find it really interesting to find this part and read on a bit further.

Words: Divil=Devil; **tight run**=close run; **logs**=ships' log-books; **paper**=newspaper; **tay**=tea; **bobby**=policeman; **widda**=widow; **clane**=clean; **allis**=always; **tin**=money; **blue**=all one's money has been spent on getting drunk; **jacket is gone etc.**=jacket is pawned; **thick**=very friendly; **trousis**=trousers.

SAILORS ASHORE

(from Betsy Lee)

Well, Divil or no, the *Hector* come home;
We raced that trip with the *Flying Foam*,
And up the river the very same tide,
And the two of them berthed there side by side;
A tight run that, and the whole of it stuck
In the paper—logs and all—good luck!
And the captain as proud, and me like a fool
Spreein' away in Liverpool—
And lodgin's of coorse, for I never could stand
Them Sailors' Homes, for a man is a man,
And a bell for dinner and a bell for tay,
And a bell to sing and a bell to pray,
And a bell for this and a bell for that,
And "Wipe your feet upon the mat!"
And the rules hung up; and fined if you're late,
And a chap like a bobby shuttin' the gate—
It isn' raisonable, it isn'
They calls it a Home, I calls it a Prison.

55

Let a man go wherever he chooses!
Ould mawther Higgins' the house that I uses—
Jem Higgins' widda—you'll be bound to know her—
Clane, but not partickiler.
There's Quiggin's too, next door but one,
Not Andrew, of coorse! but Rumpy John—
She's a dacent woman enough is Nancy,
But Higginses allis took my fancy.
There's some comfort there, for you just goes in,
And down with the watch and down with the tin,
And sleepin' and wakin', and eatin' and drinkin'—
And out and in, and never thinkin',
And carryin' on till all is blue,
And your jacket is gone and your waistcoat too.
Then of coorse you must cut your stick,
For the woman must live, however thick
You may be with her: and I'm tould there's houses
Where the people'll let ye drink your trousis;
But Higginses! never! and it isn' right!
Shirt and trousis! honour bright!

TOMMY BIG EYES

The next three poems are from Tommy Big Eyes *which is another fo'c's'le yarn told by Tom Baynes.*

TOMMY'S SCHOOLDAYS

Tommy Gelling lived on a farm north of Ramsey. He was about thirteen or fourteen, was quite ugly and was small for his age. He had eyes "as big as umbrellas" and his mother dressed him in rather babyish clothes with bits of lace at the collar and his trousers buttoned over his jacket; He looked "as though he was born to be a fool" so was often bullied by the older boys. He never complained about this; in fact, he didn't talk very much to anybody but he worked hard and and did well at school. Nellie Quine was a little girl with a fighting spirit. She was a bit younger than Tommy and she lived nearby. She would wait for Tommy when walking to or from school but, because they were both too self-conscious and shy to be seen together, Tommy and she would walk on opposite sides of the road and at some distance apart. Of course, the other children knew what was happening and they decided to tease Tommy by playing a joke on him. They persuaded him that Nelly "was desperate in love with him" and that it was time he brought her a present. Tommy did this but in Assembly that morning, events took an unforseen turn.......

Words: copies=handwriting copied onto a **slate** from excellent writing in a book or on the blackboard; **rumberella**=umbrella; **dubs**=pools; **thriven**=thrived, prospered, grown well; **briars**=wild roses; **hookin'**=turning away; **spake**=speak; **gimp**=silk or worsted cloth with wire or cord woven into the material; **quite**=quiet; **furm**=form or bench; **Bulls of Bashan**= Bashan was a kingdom near the River Jordan which was conquered by the Israelites, under Moses. It was famous for its cattle; **Hop-chu-naa** (hop-chew-nay)=cheer normally shouted on Hollantide Eve (old New Year's Eve) equivalent of Scottish "Hogmany" and is perhaps a corruption of "Hop ta'n Oie" (Hop than ee) a sort of slang meaning roughly "This is the night".

TOMMY'S SCHOOLDAYS
(from Tommy Big Eyes)

Now Tommy was as shy as a bird
"Yes" or "No" was the only word
You'd get from Tommy. So every monkey
Thought poor Tommy was a donkey.
But-bless your sowl!—lave Tommy alone!
He'd got a stunnin' head of his own;
And his copies just like copper-plate,

And he'd set to work and cover a slate
Before the rest had done a sum:
But you'd really have thought the fellow was dumb—
He was that silent and bashful, you know;
Not a fool—not him—but lookin' so.
Ugly he was, most desperate,
For all the world like a suckin' skate.
But the eyes! the eyes! Why—blow the fella!
He could spread them out like a rumberella—
You'd have wondered where on earth he got them
Deep dubs of blue light with the black at the bottom—
Basins of light. But it was very seldom
You could see them like that, for he always held them
Straight on his book or whatever he had,
As if he was ashamed, poor lad!
And really they were a most awful size;
And so we were callin' him "Tommy Big-eyes."

"Where did he come from?" did ye say?
Somewhere over Lough Molla' way;
And a road runnin' in on the opposite side,
A long sort of road that went to Kirk Bride,
And joinin' together, and leadin' down,
And over the bridge, and into the town;
And about a mile, I think it will be,
On the Kirk Bride road there's a path you'll see
Betwix' the brews that the sheep have wore.
And a cart-track leadin' to the shore;
And a pleasant little place they're callin'—
What's this it is now?—aye, "The Vollin"—
And a little house, and a garden to 't,
And a little croft, and a mackarel boat,
And some trees they've planted, but they haven't thriven,
And that's where Nelly Quine was livin'.

So you see these two would be meetin' there
Every mornin', rain or fair.
For, mind ye, if this Tommy was late—

And he tried to be—little Nelly would wait.
Wait she would, and pretend a nest,
In the briars, you know; or had to rest;
Or a pin or somethin' she was losin';
Or sittin' down to put her shoes on.
Then Tommy would come, and he'd give a peep
Round the corner, and then he'd creep
Close in to the hedge, and wouldn' allow
He saw her a bit, and on like a plough.
And there they'd go—you'd have split to seen them—
One on each side, and the road between them—
And little Nelly lookin', lookin';
And this poor bashful divil hookin'
The best he could. And every turn
In the road, no matter the bend, he'd burn
With the shame; and he'd crib himself into a O,
Like feelin' her bearin' on him, you know.
And sometimes Nelly'd give a race,
And get before him, and look in his face,
And he'd stop as dead—and she'd give a little snigger
Of a laugh in her nose, like the click of a trigger,
And lookin' under to see could she prize
His big head up with a lift of her eyes—
Botherin' this chap. But when they'd be near
The school, she wasn' willin' they'd see her
Comin' with Tommy; and she'd tuck up her clothes,
And she'd shake her hair, and away she goes;
And the little feet twinkling—ha! ha! my men!
He'd look rather sharp, would Tommy, then.

    So what did a lot of us do but join
And persuade this Tommy that Nelly Quine
Was desperate in love with him there—
And, "Spake to her, Tommy! spake to her!
Spake to her, for all!" we said:

"Yes, dyin' in love! "And he hung the head
Like a clout, poor chap! But we stuck to him still—
And "If you'll not spake, there's others that will,"
Says one of the imps. And how she'd be blushin'
When they'd tell her the bad that Tommy was wushin'
To be her sweetheart, but afraid to make free.
And listen, Tommy! the plased she'll be!"
Says the imp. Then Tommy looked up, but slow,
And the big blue eyes began to blow
Like— "Bladders" was it I was sayin'?
"Rumberellas?" Try again.
"Bubbles," was it? What d'ye call—
"Blow'n'," I said. Just aisy all!
"Blow'n'," of coorse; and the bigger the lies
The wider Tommy was spreadin' the eyes.
"She said you were handsome; she said you were smart;
She said she was almost breakin' her heart;
"She called you a duck"; "She called you a dove";
"She called you her darlin' darlin' love";
And the tasty dressed, she said she never;
And the splendid trousis he had however;
And the way they were stitched, and the beautiful gimp,
"She didn'! "says I. "She did!" says the imp:
And "Buck up, Tommy, and bring her a present."
These imps is terrible onpleasant.

So one day Tommy took the road
The very earliest he could;
And into the school as quite as a worm,
And claps his basket under the furm—
His dinner, you'd think—and waited there
Till school began; but just in the prayer
A fellow gave a shove-worse luck!
At Tommy's basket; and "Tuck-tuck-tuck!"
And the master stopped, and we all of us stopped;
And "Tuck-tuck-tuck!" and out she popped—

A beautiful little hen—and she flew
This way and that way—and "*Shish!*" and "*Shoo!*"
And over the desks; and we all gave chase,
And she flapped her wings in the master's face—
And the dignified he turned to look!
And "*Shoo!*" he says; and "Tuck-tuck-tuck"—
And away to the window, and scratched and tore;
And the feathers flyin'. "Open that door!"
Says the master then; and, glad to be shot of us,
So out goes the hen, and out goes the lot of us—
Helter-skelter, boys and gels—
Sticks and stones, or anything else
"Catch her!" "Watch her!"
"Stop her!" "Drop her!"
"Here she is!" "There she is!"
"Tommy's I'll swear she is!"
"Tommy's! Tommy's! Hop-chu-naa!
Three cheers for Tommy!—Hip-hip-hooraa!"
And a stone come flyin', and a flip and a flutter—
And down went the poor little hen in the gutter,
And her leg was broken; and "Take her up!"
And "The poor little thing!" and "Stop, then; stop!
Here's Tommy himself!" And Tommy came,
And he stood like dumb. "It's a dirty shame!"
Says one of the gels, and begun a cryin'.
Says an imp, "He brought her for Nelly Quine!"
And, "Nelly! for Nelly!" and took and caught her!
And, "Nelly's his sweetheart! It's for Nelly he brought
her!"
So when Tommy heard that, he stooped down low,
Like to take the hen, and the tears to flow
Most pitiful, and shivered all over—
And, "Look at him, Nelly! look at your lover!"
But Nelly sprung like a flash of light,
And her eye was set, and her face was white;
And she put her hand upon his head,

And, "Was it for me then, Tommy?" she said—
"Was it for me?" And he snuffs and he snivels;
And, "Yes," says Tommy. "Hooraa!" says the divils.

          Then Nelly faced round like a tiger-cat—
"You brutes!" she said, "gerr out of that!
Gerr out, you cowards!" and her face all burned
With the fury of her; and she turned,
And she took this hen that Tommy confessed,
And she coaxed it, and put it in her breast,
And kissed and kissed it over again.
"My own little hen! my own little hen!"
Says Nelly; and then she got Tommy to rise,
And took her brat to wipe his eyes.
But away goes Tommy over the street
Like the very wind, and Nelly gave sheet
As far as the bridge; but it wasn' no use,
For Tommy could run like the very deuce—
And the hen in her arms and all, you see—
So she stood and laughed; and didn't we?
Laughed and laughed—the little midge!—
And leaned against the wall of the bridge,
And laughed again; but I'll be sworn
There was many a day after that you darn'
Say much before Nelly about Tommy—no!
She wouldn't have it! Touch and go,
Was Nelly. Three words, and by jabers you'd gerrit!
Aw, the gel, ye see, had a splendid sperrit!
Just the least little *chuck!* was enough, and then
You couldn't coax her back again.
"And why did she laugh herself"—did ye say?
"The time poor Tommy was runnin' away?"
Well, everythin' of coorse in raison!
And the fool he looked, you know, was amazin'.
But, even then, when she heard us behind her,
Singin' out "Tally-high-ho-the-grinder!"

(The *grinder!* if you know what that is!)
She turned and looked like thunder at us—
And, upon my word, there's a lot of thunder
'll go in a little noddle like yonder.
So she rolled the little hen in her brat,
And its little heart all pit-a-pat—
And as dignified as dignified—
And starts, and away with her home to Kirk Bride.
And no school for her that day nor the next-
Oh, Miss Nelly was desperate vexed!

But Tommy came the very next day—
And if he didn' catch it—eh!
By gum! *He'd make an impression,*
The master said; and he gave him a threshin'
In the good old style, with your thwickumy-thwackumy!
Slishin'-slashin'! bick-o'-me-back-o'-me!
And, "Fowls!" he said. "What next?" he said—
"Ducks and geese!"—and, "Hould up your head!"—
Pigs and geese, as like as not!
Bulls of Bashan! You couldn' tell what!
The whole of the farm! "But, look ye here!"
He said—and he caught him a clip on the ear—
"You insolent vagabone!" he says,
"Who's goin' to see the end of this?
Was it fowls!! Well well! had it really come
To fowls!! Why, it abslit struck him dumb,
He said. *Of coorse,* he said, *marbles he knew,*
And even, now and then, an apple or two:
And liked his scholars to be cheerful;
But—fowls!!! he said—*it was simply fearful!*
No, he couldn', he couldn' pretend,
He really couldn', to say where would it end.
Abominable, he said, *the habits*
Of childher now-a-days!—the rabbits
And rubbish!—he said; and "Fowls!" he said—"Fowls!!"

And he lifts his voice, and reglar howls.
And the lot of us poor little blokes
Takin' care to laugh at all his jokes.
Oh! he said, *it wasn' no use!*
And down came the cane like the very deuce
By Jove! he laid into him like greens,
Till poor Tommy was all in smithereens—
The poor little chap! the way he was tanned!
But stood it grand! stood it grand!

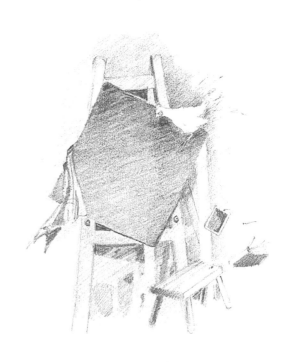

AND TOMMY HAD A FIDDLE TOO
(from Tommy Big Eyes)

When Tommy left school, he went to work as a farm labourer for Mr. and Mrs. Cain at Rensbent. Mrs. Cain was a woman who liked the farm and the house to be run in a well-ordered way. She expected the servants to be well-behaved. The poem says "She wasn' strict, so much to speak, but pitiful, and lovin' and meek". She was a kindly woman who admired Tommy's good manners and politeness. Tommy had worked harder at school than most of the other servants so he was able to read stories to them on the dark, winter nights; and Tommy had a fiddle too ....

Words: yandhar=yonder, that; **sliddher**=slip or slide; **onaisy**= uneasy.

AND TOMMY HAD A FIDDLE TOO
(from Tommy Big Eyes)

And Tommy had a fiddle too,
And I don't know what was there he couldn' do
With yandhar fiddle, the way it'd mock
Everything—it'd crow like a cock,
It'd hoot like a donkey, it'd moo like a cow;
It'd cry like a baby, it'd grunt like a sow,
Or a thrush, or a pigeon, or a lark, or a linnet—
You'd really thought they were livin' in it.
But the tunes he was playin'—that was the thing
Like squeezin' honey from the string;
Like milkin' a fiddle—no jerks, no squeaks—
And the tears upon the misthress' cheeks.
And sometimes he'd play a dance—and what harm!
But she wouldn' have it upon the farm,
The misthress wouldn'—dancin', I mean—
It didn' matter so much for the play'n':
But she'd often stop him, and ask would he change
To a nice slow tune, and Tommy would range
Up and down the strings, and sliddher
Into the key; and then he'd feather
The bow very fine, and a sort of a hum,

Like a bee round a flower, and out it'd come—
"Ould Robin Gray," or the "Lover's Ghost"—
That's the two she liked the most:
And the gels, that only a minute afore
Were ready to jump and clear the floor,
Sat still on the form, but onaisy though,
And terr'ble disappointed, you know.
And sometimes they'd be coaxin' Tommy to take
The fiddle out in the orchard, and shake
His funny-bone over a jig or a reel—
Something to tickle a body's heel,
Says one of the gels—and "I'll give you a kiss!
Faith, I will then, Tommy!" she says:
And Tommy that blushed to the roots of his hair;
But still, he said, *"no matter where,*
If the misthress wasn' willing,
He wouldn'—and, "Tommy, we'll give you a shillin'!"
And coaxin' away: but he didn' regard them.
And anyway, you know, she'd have heard them.

BACK'S FUGES *(few jez)*
(from Tommy Big Eyes)

Mr. Cain was a local preacher as well as being Tommy's employer. He told him to stop playing the violin and learn to play the bass-viol for the Methodist chapel services but Tommy wouldn't do this until he'd first had a word with the vicar. The vicar was a very cultured Englishman whose education had started at a choir school. He had a piano at the vicarage and soon Tommy and he were playing duets together until the early hours of the morning. To help him practise at home, the vicar lent Tommy a big music book full of Fugues by Johann Sebastian Bach. This extract from Tommy Big Eyes deserves a place in any music text book which tries to explain what a fugue is.

Words: register=book kept in church recording all the births, marriages and deaths in the parish; **Back**=Bach; **swivel**=swerving; **give it him**=reprimand him, tell him off; **rejisin**=rejoicing.

BACK'S   FUGES
(from Tommy Big Eyes)

So Tommy come home, and a book at him there
As big as the parish register—
Somewhere about the weight of a sack
Of potatoes, and every bit of it Back—
Back! yes, Back—you don't know what I mean?
Of coorse, of coorse! Well, you see, I'll explain—
Tommy that was tellin' me,
And showin' the way, and how would it be.
Well, it's a diffficult sort of music, look'ee!
Slantindicular, that is, crooky,
Up and down, in and out—
Bless me! what am I talkin' about!
Complercated—heads and tails—
Scientific, that is, scales—
I don't know whether you've ever heard—
Fidgets, fuges! that's the word—
Fuges, fuges, that's what I meant—
Excellent, though, excellent!
Fidgets—good! but avast them nudges!
I'm goin' to tell you what a fudge is—
Fuge—dear heart!
What a start!
Well, obsarve! away goes a scrap,
Just a piece of a tune, like a little chap
That runs from his mammy; but mind the row
There'll be about that chap just now!
Off he goes! but whether or not,
The mother is after him like a shot—
Run, you rascal, the fast you're able!
But she nearly nabs him at the gable;
But missin' him after all: and then
He'll give her the imperince of sin:
And he'll duck and he'll dive, and he'll dodge and he'll dip
And he'll make a run, and he'll give her the slip,
And back again, and turnin' and mockin',

67

And imitatin' her most shockin',
Every way she's movin', you know
That's just the way this tune'll go;
Imitatin', changin', hidin',
Doublin' upon itself, dividin':
And other tunes comin' wantin' to dance with it,
But haven't the very smallest chance with it—
It's that slippy and swivel—up, up, up!
Down, down, down! the little pup—
Friskin', whiskin'; and then as solemn,
Like marchin' in a double column,
Like a funeral: or, rather,
If you'll think of this imp, it's like the father
Comin' out to give it him, and his heavy feet
Soundin' like thunder on the street.
And he's caught at last, and they all sing out
Like the very mischief, and dance and shout,
And caper away there most surprisin',
And ends in a terrible rejisin'.
That's Backs, that's fuges—aw, that's fine—
But never mind! never mind!

THE DOCTOR and THE SCHOOLMASTERS

There are ten fo'c's'le yarns narrated by Tom Baynes, and we have chosen excerpts from four of them. The Schoolmasters *is the last of our choices.*

WHITEWASH, CHOLERA AND MIDDENS
(from The Doctor)

Very few Manx villages escaped the ravages of the Cholera epedemic which swept through the Island in 1832 and in which thousands of people died. The Brown family had just moved from Douglas to Braddan at the time. T. E. Brown was only two years old then, and no-one in the Brown family was affected. He cannot have remembered cholera but must have been told of its horrors many times so he was able to write of its terrible effects in The Doctor.

In the poem, Tom Baynes does not remember the epedemic either and recalls only what he has been told about the disease coming to Brown's imaginary village called The Lhen; this is the village mentioned in Betsy Lee *where Pazon Gale, Doctor Bell and the Baynes and Lee families lived.*

Words: texes=texts (short excerpts, normally from the Bible, used by preachers to reinforce moral messages in their sermons); **mustn'**=must not; **middens**=dung heap usually sited in the middle of the farmyard; **little sup**=little drop of alcoholic drink; **strooghed**=stroked; **clane**=clean; **capers**=folly.

WHITEWASH, CHOLERA AND MIDDENS
(from The Doctor)

And had a meetin' up at the school,
And the Pazon there; and Master Coole
That was Captain of the Parish was there;
And of coorse the captain would be in the chair,
But couldn' put out no talk at all;
And then the people gave a call
For the Docthor to spake, and so he did,
But the Pazon first. And the little he said
Was very good. And *The Lord had sent*
The cholera for them to repent
And call upon His name, and turn!
He said; *and His anger wouldn' burn*
For ever, he said. *And Our sins was great;*
But come unto the mercy seat!
He said, and the crimson would be like the wool!—
Aw, capital texes! Beautiful!
So I was tould at them that heard—
And the Docthor didn' say a word
Against the Pazon, but bowin', though,
And, "Our respected vicar," you know—
And that. Aw, bless ye! these Englishmen
Can do it with a taste they can—
Chut! of coorse! and readier far!
The Manx is awkward! yes, they are!
And excellent advise! and trustin'
They'd never forget; but for all they mustn'

69

Lave everythin' to the Lord, and sit
With their hands before them; but help a bit
Theirselves. And wouldn' the Lord be willin'
Of a bit of whitewash goin' a spillin'
About the place? And what would they say
To begin and clear the middens away?

 And then an ould fisherman got up
(I believe he had a little sup),
And strooghed the hair, the way with them chaps,
And a little spit and a little cough perhaps—
And says he, "The whitewash'll do very well—
But middens is middens, Masther Bell!"
He says. Aw, bless us! the laugh that was there!
"Middens is middens!" Aw dear, aw dear!
Billy Sayle they were callin' him,
But he was never gettin' no other name
After that but "Billy the Midden."
And they wouldn' clane them; and they didn'!
And of coorse they were right! What nonsense—bless ye!
Them docthors, they're fit enough to disthress ye!
Capers! What's more comfortable
Till a midden about a house, if you're able
To have a midden, and keep it nice,
And anyways dry? And think of the price
Of dung and potatoes? You can't do without them;
And how will you be doin' about them
If you hav'n' a midden! Chut! they're clever,
But hasn' the smallest notion whatever
About dung—not them! And as for the stink—
A midden needn' be a sink!
Trim it nice upon the street,
And a midden'll smell as sweet as sweet,
And very wholesome. I know it depends
Altogether on who attends
To the lek, and careful in the spreddin';
But of coorse a man'll be proud of his midden.

ROLL CALL OF THE DEAD
(from The Doctor)

Because we are only talking about a number, it doesn't really mean very much to us when we hear that "thousands died". But this extract from The Doctor *makes us realize that those "thousands" were real people. Listing the dead from this one village in this way helps us realize just how terrible the tragedy was that hit the Island in those far-off days.*

Words: Ax=*ask;* **lek**=*like, probably.*

ROLL CALL OF THE DEAD
(from The Doctor)

Well, the whitewash done a power of good,
And slishin' it everywhere they could;
Till, one way or another the sickness broke,
And then they were countin' who was took—
Just like after a battle, they're sayin',
They're goin' about to count the slain.
There was two at Cleator's, and two at Gick's,
And two at Corkhill's—that'd be six—
And three at Kewin's, and Shimmin's four,
Well, now, that'll be seven more;
And six and seven'll be thirteen,
And a baby took at Tommy Cregeen:
And Jemmy Cregeen he lost a son,
And Juan Quayle, and Nelly Bun,
And a boy of Callow's, and three of Creer's—
Gels, I think—and at Harry Tear's
There wasn' a soul in the house alive,
So that'll be makin' twenty-five.
But that wasn' all. I tell ye, then,
There was forty people dead at the Lhen.
I don't know was I born or not
Them times myself; but that's the lot!
That's the number they were tellin'
And no mistake. Ax Neddy Crellin!
All in a month, aye, every man of them!
And never no stone put up to the one of them,
No time, I tell ye, nor money, it's lek.
How could ye expec'? How could ye expec'?

71

THE BATTLE OF WATERLOO
(from The Schoolmasters)

Waterloo, in Belgium, was the site of one of the most famous and ferocious battles in British history when, in 1815, the Duke of Wellington's armies defeated Napoleon Bonaparte for the final time. Afterwards, the expression "Battle of Waterloo" came to mean a really awful - and possibly violent - quarrel. This is what is recorded in this extract from The Schoolmasters. *Once more Tom Baynes is telling of his childhood as he reveals both the inadequacies of Danny Bewidher's teaching and the violence which is sometimes aroused in his mother. Like many another mother before and since, she doesn't wait for a reason to clout Tom on the head but she is not prepared to let the schoolmaster hurt him.*

Words: laste=least; **bogh**=useless fool;   **kyout** (one syllable)=miserable creature; **sniffikin**=insignificant; **Archdakin**=archdeacon (clergyman next in rank below a bishop); **spakin'**=speaking; **'deed**=indeed; **turns me up**=upside-down to show bruises on buttocks; **inkstand**=wooden or metal holder for a pot of ink; **my annim=**upon my soul;   **urrov**=out of; **rowlin'** ("row" rhymes with "cow")=rolling;   **furrims**=forms, benches;   **stuck to him manful**=kept hold of him manfully;   **fac'**=fact; **birch**=birch twigs bound together for beating people on the buttocks; **strap**=for beating across the hand.

THE BATTLE OF WATERLOO
(from The Schoolmasters)

But the school at the Lhen was just for childher,
Enfan's in perricuts—Danny Bewildher
Was the name of the Master, callin' him out
Of his proper name, that was Danny the Spout;
At laste—I don't know; but Skillicorn,
I've heard them sayin', the man was born—
Poor old Dan—aw, bless your sowl!—
Now was it Skillicorn, or Cowle?
Aw dear!

Aw, little things thim times: but grew,
Till at last the battle of Waterloo
Betwix' my mother and Danny, that plied me
With the cane one day till he nearly destroyed me.
And home I run, and—"Mother! mother!"

72

And—"Dan hev kilt me!" And—"What's this bother?"
And takes and hits me a clout on the head,
And looks me all over, and "Come!" she said.
And away with me there; and in on the school—
 And—"What's this," she says, "ye dirty fool?
Ye bogh! ye kyout ye! *you* a man?
You sniffikin' creep!" she says to Dan—
"You?" and just a disgrace
To the place—
And the Bishop and the Archdakin—
Aye—and she'd be spakin'
To the Pazon—'deed she'd let him know!
She would so!
And pins him theer against the wall,
And turns me up, and shows him all.

  "Gerr out!" says Dan; "Gerr out!" says he.
"Is it *out?*" she says, and droppin' me,
"Is it *out?*" and grips an inkstand there,
And ups and lets him have it fair
Betwix' the eyes—aw, the ink and the blood!
And Danny all smotherin' where he stood,
And puffin' and blowin', and spatt'rin' and sputt'rin',
And all the dirt goin' sloppin' and gutt'rin'
Down his breast, and—*his shirt?* my annim!
Never had the lek upon him,
Nor the name o' the lek.

  "Gerr urrov this school!"
Says Dan, and makes a grab at a stool,
And a run and a drive, and she couldn' recover her
Footin', and down, and Danny over her!
So there they were rowlin', and crish! crash!
And the furrims capsized, and mixed in a mash
Of murder—bless ye! stuck to him manful—
Aye, and handful after handful
Of Danny's hair went flyin' about;

73

And the childher all began to shout,
The boys to cheer, and the gels to cry;
And then I come behind on the sly,
And caught this Danny a clip on the ear,
And he turned, and she saw her chance, and got clear,
And up and off with us—aw, it's a fac'—
And left poor Danny on his back.

     Well, then I was goin' to school at the Church,
To Clukish himself, that was usin' a birch,
But very little, or a leather strap—
But mostly he was givin' ye a rap
On the head with his knuckles—and a little *hem!*
Aw, a grand ould man was Jemmy Jem.

LYRICAL POEMS

T. E. Brown's works are not widely known off the Island. This is probably because so many of them were written in the Manx dialect and are therefore not easy for non-Manx people to read. When, in 1893, just four years before he died, he published Old John and Other Poems *which were all written in standard English, the book sold well and thousands of people who had found his earlier works difficult enjoyed his poetry for the first time. Some of the* Old John *poems are amongst the ones which follow.*

The term "lyric" comes from the word "lyre" which was a stringed musical instrument used by the ancient Greeks to accompany their songs. Strictly speaking, lyric poetry is simple, expresses personal feelings and is written in rhyming groups of lines called stanzas and it lends itself to being sung. Lyric poetry should not include set forms such as sonnets or ballads but, in modern times, scholars who feel that poems simply have *to be classified have dubbed any poem "lyric" which they have been unable to group under any other heading.*

The compilers of The Collected Poems of T. E. Brown *did this and we have followed their example.*

CLIFTON

Brown was Second Master (Vice-Principal) at Clifton College at Bristol. There is plenty of evidence that he was contented there for he loved the countryside and he had a very happy family life. However, like most people, he found his work monotonous at times and we know from his letters that he always kept his work and his private thoughts well separated.

It is thought that he wrote Clifton *in his last year of teaching. He was sixty years of age, his health had been poor, his wife had died three years earlier and retirement was looming. He was probably having an "off" day and feeling intensely the exile's painful longing for the isle of his birth.*

Words: thrice=three times (i.e. 3 x 9 years=27 years); **squad**=this might be a reference to the Officers' Training Corps (core) at Clifton in which Brown was an instructor; **pragmatic**=meddlesome; **bate**=Victorian schoolboy slang word meaning "rage" or "temper". These last two words are nouns but Brown is using "bate" as a verb here; **lichens** (lichens not likens)=minute green, grey or yellow vegetable growth on stones, rocks and tree-trunks.

See also: Epistola ad Dakyns (p.77).

CLIFTON

I'm here at Clifton, grinding at the mill
    My feet for thrice nine barren years have trod;
But there are rocks and waves at Scarlett still,
    And gorse runs riot in Glen Chass—thank God!

Alert, I seek exactitude of rule,
    I step, and square my shoulders with the squad;
But there are blaeberries on old Barrule,
    And Langness has its heather still—thank God!

There is no silence here the truculent quack
    Insists with acrid shriek my ears to prod,
And, if I stop them, fumes; but there's no lack
    Of silence still on Carraghyn—thank God!

Pragmatic fibs surround my soul, and bate it
    With measured phrase, that asks the assenting nod;
I rise, and say the bitter thing, and hate it-
    But Wordsworth's castle's still at Peel—thank God!

O broken life! O wretched bits of being,
    Unrhythmic, patched, the even and the odd!
But Bradda still has lichens worth the seeing,
    And thunder in her caves-thank God! thank God!

EPISTOLA AD DAKYNS

The title is in Latin and means Letter to Dakyns. *H. G. Dakyns was a teaching colleague and close friend of Brown at Clifton. Brown was godfather to Dakyns's son. The introductory stanza states that after Brown dies his spirit will haunt the places which he loved and Dakyns will be able to feel Brown's presence there.*

This view demonstrates Brown's uncertainty about the form our afterlife will take as it does not entirely accord with his portrayal of eternity as revealed in other poems. The stanza numbered I *shows us that Brown really loved the Avon Gorge near the college at Clifton where he frequently walked the cliff paths before work in the early mornings of summer. The stanza numbered* II *reveals similar feelings for the English Lake District around Keswick but that numbered* III *reveals the Isle of Man to be the place "God keeps for me".*

Words: What I meant=what my life meant; **natherless**=nevertheless; **earth, air, fire, sea** (water)=Aristotle's four "elements" of nature; **wraith**=a person's "double" supposedly seen shortly after death; **great Master's rhythmic feet**=perhaps an association with Blake's idea that Jesus had walked in England; **coeval**=existing at the same time; **wampum**=polished beads; **anthithesis**=opposite thought or system; **kern**=cairn; **"sure and certain hope"**=eternal life; **a bud so rare**=Amy Dora, Brown's baby daughter buried in Maughold churchyard; **vows I vowed**=marriage vows (Brown was married in Maughold Church).

See also: Clifton *(p. 75); Letters of Thomas Edward Brown* edited by Sydney T. Irwin (for Brown's opinions about eternal life).

EPISTOLA AD DAKYNS

DAKYNS, when I am dead,
Three places must by you be visited,
Three places excellent,
Where you may ponder what I meant,
And then pass on—
Three places you must visit when I'm gone.
Yes, *meant*, not *did*, old friend!
For neither you nor I shall see the end,
And do the thing we wanted:
Natheless three places will be haunted
By what of me

The earth and air
Shall spare,
And fire and sea
Let be—
Three places only,
Three places, Dakyns.

I

The first is by the Avon's side,
Where tall rocks flank the winding tide.
There come when morning's virgin kiss
Awakes from dreams the clematis,
And every thorn and briar is set
As with a diamond coronet—
There come, and pause upon the edge,
And I will lean in every ledge,
And melt in grays, and flash in whites,
And linger in a thousand lights;
And yield in bays, and urge in capes,
And fill the old familiar shapes;
And yearn in curves, and strain to meet
The pensive pressure of your feet
And you shall feel an inner sense,
A being kindred and intense;
And you shall feel a strict control,
A something drawing at your soul,
A going out, a life suspended,
A spirit with a spirit blended.
And you shall start as from a dream,
While I, withdrawing down the stream,
Drift vaporous to the ancient sea,
A wraith, a film, a memory—
Three places, Dakyns.

II

The next is where a hundred fells
Stand round the Lake like sentinels,

Where Derwent, like a sleeping beauty,
Girdled with that watchful duty,
At Skiddaw's foot securely lies,
And gives her bosom to the skies.
O, come! and I will bid the moon
All subtle harmonies attune
That live in shadows and in heights,
A mystic chorus of delights.
O, come where many an Island bevels
It's strand to meet the golden levels!
O, lay your heart upon each line,
So diamond-cut and crystalline,
That seams the marble of the mere,
And smoothes all troubles, calms all fear,
With that sweet natural straightness, free
From effort or inconstancy.
O, draw your thought with all its passion
Along the melancholy fashion
Of forms accentuate with the beat
Of the great Master's rhythmic feet.
But when upon the finest verge
The sense no further flight can urge,
When the full orb of contemplation
Is stretched, a nameless tribulation
Shall sway the whole, a silent stress
Borne in upon that loveliness;
A burden as of human ills,
A human trouble in the hills;
A quickening pulse in earth and sky,
And you shall know that it is I—
Three places, Dakyns.

III

The next is where God keeps for me
A little island in the sea,
A body for my needs, that so
I may not all unclothed go,

79

A vital instrument whereby
I still may commune with the sky,
When death hath loosed the plaited strands,
And left me feeling for the lands.
Even now between its simple poles
It has the soul of all my souls.
But then—whatever I have been,
Whatever felt, whatever seen,
Whatever guessed, or understood,
The tones of right, the tints of good,
The loves, the hates, the hopes, the fears,
The gathered strength of all my years—
All that my life has in me wrought
Of complex essence shall be brought
And wedded to those primal forms
That have their scope in calms and storms,
Attunéd to the swells and falls
Of Nature's holy intervals.
And, old coeval use surviving,
No need shall be for any striving,
No need from point to point to press,
And swell the growing consciousness,
But in a moment I shall sit
Sphered in the very heart of it.
And every hill from me shall shoot,
And spread as from a central root,
And every crag and every spur,
To me its attitude refer;
And I shall be the living heart,
And I shall live in every part,
With elemental cares engrossed,
And all the passions of the coast.
Come then, true Dakyns, be the test
Most meet to make me manifest!
Come, and immediate recognise
To all your moods the dumb replies.
Or stretch across a kindly void

The golden life-chords unalloyed
With thought, and instant they shall wake
The music they were made to make.
Thus shall you grow into a sense
Of islandhood, not taking thence
Some pretty surfaces and angles,
Tricking your soul, as with fine spangles
A savage studs its wampum belt,
But patient till the whole is felt,
And you become incorporate
Into and undivided state.
Then shall your body be as dead;
And you shall take to you instead
The system of the natural powers,
The heath that blooms, the cloud that lowers,
The antithesis of things that bide,
The cliff, the beach, the rock, the tide—
The lordly things, whose generous feud
Is but a fixed vicissitude.
Wherefore, O Maughold, if he come,
If Dakyns come,
Let not a voice be dumb
In any cave;
Fling up the waves
In wreaths of giddy spray;
O'er all the bay
Flame out in gorse around the "kern,"
And let his heart within him burn,
Until he gains the slope
Where, in the "sure and certain hope,"
Sleep the long rows:
Then let him quench the fiery gleams,
Of Death's gray shadow of repose,
As one who dreams
He knows not what, and yet he knows
I have her there
That was a bud so rare.

But, Bradda, if he come to you,
I charge you to be true!
Sit not all sullen by the sea,
But show that you are conscious it is he.
It is no vulgar tread
That bends the heath:
Broad be the heavens spread
Above, the sea beneath
Blue with *that* blue!
And let the whispering airs
Move in the ferns. By those strong prayers
Which rent my heart that day as lightening rents a cloud,
And rips it till it glares
To open view: by all the vows I vowed,
I charge you, and I charge you by the tears
And by the passion that I took
From you, and flung them to the vale,
And had the ultimate vision, do not fail!
Three places only—
Three places, Dakyns.

Clifton, *December* 1869.

CHALSE Y KILLEY

Chalse Gell was a simple-minded, wandering preacher. He had the habit of turning up at people's houses expecting to be fed and housed, but he was welcomed as a "character" who was both humorous and sincere. He railed against alcoholic drinks and Roman Catholics. He also protested strongly against the enclosure of common land and the consequent removal of the commoner's ancient grazing rights. T. E. Brown remembered him from his childhood and he wrote this poem at Port Erin in 1875 when he heard that Chalse had died.

The full poem has ten verses but there are only three of them here. They show that Charles was not so simple that he couldn't make fools of a bunch of cheeky boys.

Words: Chalse ('a' as in apple)=Charles; **Y Killey** (kill'ya)=of the church; **unweeting**=unwitting; **palpable typology**="concrete" interpretation or "seeing for ourselves".

CHALSE A KILLEY:
To Chalse in Heaven

So you are gone, dear Chalse!
Ah! well: it was enough—
The ways were cold, the ways were rough—
O Heaven! O home!
No more to roam—
Chalse, poor Chalse.

And now it's all so plain, dear Chalse!
So plain—
The wildered brain,
The joy, the pain—
The phantom shapes that haunted,
The half-born thoughts that daunted—
All, all is plain
Dear Chalse! All is plain.
Yet where you're now, dear Chalse,
Have you no memory
Of land and sea,
Of vagrant liberty?
Through all your dreams

83

Come there no gleams
Of morning sweet and cool
On old Barrule?
Breathes there no breath,
Far o'er the hills of Death,
Of a soft wind that dallies
Among the Curragh sallies—
Shaking the perfumed gold-dust on the streams?
Chalse, poor Chalse!

Great joy was yours, dear Chalse! when first I met you
In that old Vicarage
That shelters under Bradda: we did get you
By stratagem most sage:
Of youthful mischief—got you all unweeting
Of mirthful toys—
A merry group of girls and boys,
To hold a missionary meeting;
And you did stand upon a chair,
In the best parlour there;
And dear old Parson Corrin was from home,
And I did play a tune upon a comb;
And unto us
You did pronounce a speech most marvellous,
Dear Chalse! and then you said
And *sthrooghed* the head—
"If there'll be no objection,
We'll now *purseed* to the collection"—
Chalse, poor Chalse!

And do you still remember, Chalse,
How at the Dhoor—
Near Ramsey, to be sure—
I got two painters painting in the chapel
To make with me a congregation?
And you did mount the pulpit, and did grapple
With a tremendous text, and warn the nation

84

Of drunkenness; and in your hand
Did wave an empty bottle, so that we,
By palpable typology,
Might understand—
Dear Chalse, you never had!
An audience more silent or more sad!

THE PEEL LIFEBOAT

If you go to Peel Lifeboat House, you can see "George", a massive figurehead which was retrieved from the wreckage of the St. George. She was a Norwegian sailing ship which foundered against the cliffs of Peel Hill in a terrible storm on the 7th. October, 1889, just eight years before the death of T. E. Brown.

There were no motor lifeboats in those days and, with the ferocious storm blowing straight into Peel, it was impossible to use the lifeboat's sail. Charlie Cain, the coxswain (cox'n) of the Peel lifeboat—the John Monk—headed into the wild seas with sixteen brave crewmen, twelve of whom were manning the heavy oars.

It took two hours of solid effort for the lifeboat to reach the doomed ship which was already beginning to break up, littering the waves with spars and broken planks, so that it was too dangerous to go alongside. However, a line was passed between the two vessels and rescue of the twenty-three souls on board began. First to be hauled over was Mrs. Thorensen, wife of the St. George's captain, and she was followed by the ship's carpenter who had a canvas bag strapped to his back. The lifeboat crew were not immediately keen to take "luggage" on board but soon realised that the bag contained Sigrid, the Thorensens' nine month old baby daughter. Everyone from the St. George was safely landed in Peel and within the hour the vessel was smashed to pieces. For this heroic rescue, each crew member received a silver medal from Norway and T. E. Brown wrote this dramatic, rhythmical poem which has deservedly immortalised the rescue.

The Thorensen family have maintained contact with Peel ever since and in 1989, one hundred years after the rescue, Mrs. Karin Nordli—baby Sigrid's daughter—presented a cheque of £3,000 to the Peel Lifeboat Ladies' Guild to help with the costs of refurbishing the lifeboat house.

Words: gorge=throat; **in swound**=having fainted.

THE PEEL LIFEBOAT

Of Charley Cain, the cox,
And the thunder of the rocks,
And the ship *St. George*—
How he balked the sea-wolf's gorge
Of its prey—
Southward bound from Norraway;
And the fury and the din,
And the horror and the roar,
Rolling in, rolling in,
Rolling in upon the dead lee-shore!

See the Harbour-master stands,
Cries—"Have you all your hands?"
Then, as an angel springs
With Gods breath upon his wings,
She went;
And the black storm robe was rent
With the shout and with the din....

And the castle walls were crowned,
And no woman lay in swound,
But they stood upon the height
Straight and stiff to see the fight,
For they knew
What the pluck of men can do:
With the fury and the din....

"Lay aboard her, Charley lad!"
"Lay aboard her!—Are you mad?
With the bumping and the scamper
Of all this loose deck hamper,
And the yards
Dancing round us here like cards,"
With the fury and the din....

So Charley scans the rout,
Charley knows what he's about,
Keeps his distance, heaves the line—
"Pay it out there true and fine!
Not too much, men!
Take in the slack, you Dutchmen!"
With the fury and the din....

Now the hauser's fast and steady,
And the traveller rigged and ready.
Says Charley—"Whats the lot?"
"Twenty-four." Then like a shot—
"Twenty-three,"
Says Charley, "'s all I see"—
With the fury and the din....

"Not a soul shall leave the wreck,"
Says Charley, "till on deck
You bring the man that's hurt."
So they brought him in his shirt—
O, it's fain
I am for you, Charles Cain—
With the fury and the din....

And the Captain and his wife,
And a baby! Odds my life!
Such a beauty! Such a prize!
And the tears in Charley's eyes.
Arms of steel,
For the honour of old Peel
Haul away amid the din....

Sing ho! the seething foam!
Sing ho! the road for home!

And the hulk they've left behind,
Like a giant stunned and blind
With the loom
And the boding of his doom—
With the fury and the din....

"Here's a child! dont let it fall!"
Says Charley, "Nurse it, all!"
O the tossing of the breasts!
O the brooding of soft nests,
Taking turns,
As each maid and mother yearns
For the babe that 'scaped the din...

See the rainbow bright and broad!
Now, all men, thank ye God,
For the marvel and the token
And The word that He hath spoken!
With Thee,
O Lord of all that be,
We have peace amid the din,
And the horror and the roar,
Rolling in, rolling in,
Rolling in upon the dead lee-shore.

THE PESSIMIST or
THE RAVEN AND THE JACKDAW

Two characters are speaking and showing two very different views on life.

If you and a friend say this poem out aloud you might form some ideas of your own as to why T. E. Brown chose this way of expressing these thoughts.

Words: pessimist=person who always takes a gloomy view of events; **tyrant**=a cruel ruler; **d—d**=when T. E. Brown wrote this poem it would have been thought rude to have written in the missing letters.

THE PESSIMIST or
THE RAVEN AND THE JACKDAW

"CROAK—croak—croak!
Life's a pig-in-a-poke."
"Indeed!" says the little Jackdaw.

"Croak—croak—croak!
And a cruel joke!"
"Dear me!" says the little Jackdaw.

"Croak—croak—croak!
It's a tyrant's yoke!"
"How?" says the little Jackdaw.

"Croak—croak—croak!
We must vanish like smoke."
"Why?" says the little Jackdaw.

"Croak—croak—croak!
Ask the elm! ask the oak!"
"What?" says the little Jackdaw.

"Croak—croak—croak!
Your feelings you cloke!"
"Where?" says the little Jackdaw.

"Croak—croak—croak!
Do you like your own folk?"
"Yes!" says the little Jackdaw.

"Croak—croak—croak!
With despair don't you choke?"
"No!" says the little Jackdaw.

"Croak—croak—croak!
You're a d—d little bloke!"
"Always was" says the little Jackdaw.

THE   INTERCEPTED   SALUTE

There is a saying which states that if someone in London smiles at the bus conductor as they hand over their fare, within two hours "the smile will have reached more than a million people". What it assumes is that the conductor will smile at the next passenger who, in turn, will smile at the next person she/he meets and before long everyone around is smiling. You might like to think of this story when reflecting on The Intercepted Salute. *There are other points to think about as well; for instance, T. E. Brown implies that people mellow as they grow older. Is this true? Also, nowadays children are urged "not to talk to strangers" wheras, until recently, it was considered to be very bad-mannered if you did not make strangers feel welcome. Children and adults in the street were all expected to greet people, particularly those that they did not know, with a polite "Good Morning" or other salutation. T. E. Brown wrote this poem at Coniston in the English Lake District, in July 1869.*

Words: **fain**=with pleasure;   **wrought**=worked;   **sober**=real or less exciting; **manifest**=obvious.

THE INTERCEPTED SALUTE

A LITTLE maiden met me in the lane,
And smiled a smile so very fain,
So full of trust and happiness,
I could not choose but bless
The child, that she should have such grace
To laugh into my face.

She never could have known me; but I thought
It was the common joy that wrought
Within the little creature's heart,
As who should say:—"Thou art
As I; the heaven is bright above us;
And there is God to love us.
And I am but a little gleeful maid,
And thou art big, and old, and staid;
But the blue hills have made thee mild
As is a little child.
Wherefore I laugh that thou may'st see—
O, laugh! O, laugh with me!"
A pretty challenge! Then I turned me round,
And straight the sober truth I found.
For I was not alone; behind me stood,
Beneath his load of wood,
He that of right the smile possessed—
Her father manifest.

O, blest be God! that such an overplus
Of joy is given to us:
That that sweet innocent
Gave me the gift she never meant,
A gift secure and permanent!
For, howsoe'er the smile had birth,
It is an added glory on the earth.

"NOT WILLING TO STAY"

Poetry allows the reader to interpret the words in his/her own way and "Not Willing to Stay" demonstrates this attribute very well. We are not told what the relationship is between the "fisher bold", Evan, and the child in this poem; amongst all the detail, the only hard pieces of information are that the child the poet had known some time previously had been not willing to stay and that Evan is prepared to say that and nothing more. You might like to discuss this poem with other people; why, for instance, has the poet written the words "not willing to stay" as an actual quotation in inverted commas in the title and when they appear again in the next to last line. They only exist in the poet's mind at that point and are not said aloud.

Could there be a concealed meaning to the words and, if so, what might that meaning be? Why will the "fisher bold" tell the enquirer so little? Can you think of any reasons why she should wish to leave or where she might have gone to? Did she really want to go or is that just Evan's version of events? Do you think that the girl was one of the his relations and if they were related does this affect your interpretation of the words?

If this poem is based on a real event, the characters are probably not Manx as it was written when Brown was holidaying at St. Bees Head in Cumberland during August 1868.

Words: yestreen= yesterday evening; **blithesome**=joyous; **the May**=may (hawthorne) blossom; **brae** (bray)= steep slope or grassy bank.

See also: Fives'-Court (p.117).

"NOT WILLING TO STAY"

I SAW a fisher bold yestreen
  At his cottage by the bay,
And I asked how he and his had been,
  While I was far away.
But when I asked him of the child
  With whom I used to play,
The sunniest thing that ever smiled
  Upon a summer's day—
Then said that fisher bold to me—
  And turned his face away:—
"She was not willing to stay with us—
  She was not willing to stay."

"But, Evan, she was brave and strong,
  And blithesome as the May;
And who would do her any wrong,
  Our darling of the bay?"
His head was low, his breath was short,
  He seemed as he would pray,
Nor answer made in any sort
  That might his grief betray;
Save once again that fisher bold
  Turned, and to me did say:—
"She was not willing to stay with us,
  She was not willing to stay."

Then I looked upon his pretty cot,
  So neat in its array,
And I looked upon his garden-plot
  With its flowers so trim and gay;
And I said—"He hath no need of me
  To help him up the brae;
God worketh in his heart, and He
  Will soon let in the day."
So I left him there, and sought yon rock
  Where leaps the salt sea-spray;
For ah! how many have lost their loves
That were "not willing to stay" with them,
  That were not willing to stay!

CATHERINE KINRADE

READ THESE NOTES BEFORE READING THE POEM.

None of T. E. Brown's poems better reveals his hummanity, understanding of human frailties and recognition that Christianity means forgiveness than this poem does.

Catherine Kinrade is written of a time in the early eighteenth century when the "Great" Bishop Wilson had restored the Ecclesiastical (church) Courts in the Island. These heard charges against people who had not necessarily broken any of Tynwald's laws but who were charged with breaking the laws of the established church. The judges were clergymen; usually one of three Vicars-General, along with the Bishop of Sodor and Man. "Purging" was a common punishment, particularly for people who had relationships with the opposite sex when they were not married and these purgings were very harsh. The Church's Consistory Court twice severely punished Catherine Kinrade, although it knew she was mentally disabled. Below, we have printed copies of documents which were written at the time and you will see that Bishop Wilson, himself, signed the Orders for Catherine's punishments.

Extract from *Manx Society's Publications, vol. xi.* pp. 98, 99:

"ANOTHER unfortunate creature was soon afterwards subjected to the same treatment, although it was admitted she had 'a degree of unsettledness and defect of understanding,' and, as was certified by the clergy, that she had submitted 'with as much submission and discretion as can be expected of the like of her,' and 'considering the defect of her understanding.' The records state—'Forasmuch as neither Christian advice nor gentle modes of punishment are found to have any effect on Kath. Kinred of Kirk Christ, a notorious strumpet, who had brought forth three illegitimate children, and still continues to stroll about the country, and lead a most vicious and scandalous life on other accounts; all which tending to the great dishonour of the Christian name, and to her own utter destruction without a timely and thorough reformation. It is there-fore hereby ordered (as well for the further punishment of the said delinquent as for the example of others) that the said Kath. Kinred be dragged after a boat in the sea at Peel, on Wed., the 17th inst. (being the fair of St. Patrick), at the height of the market. To which end, a boat and boat's crew are to be charged by the general sumner, and the constable and soldiers of the garrison are, by the Governor's order, to be aiding and assisting in seeing this censure performed. And in case any owner, master, or crew of any boat are found refractory, by refusing or neglecting to per-form this service for the restraining of vice, their names are to be forthwith given in by the general sumner, to the end they may be severally fined for their contempt, as the Governor's order directs. Dated at Bishop's Court this 15th day of March, 1713.

' THOS. SODOR AND MAN.
' WILLIAM WALKER'.

"It was certified by the Sumner General so long after as July 13th ensuing, that 'St. Patrick's day being so stormy and tempestuous that no boat could perform the within censure, upon St.German's day about the height of the market the within Kath. Kinred was dragged after a boat in the sea according to the within order. ' However, poor Katherine Kinred is not yet done with, for on the 27th Oct., 1718, having had a fourth bastard Child, and 'after imprisonment, penance, dragging in the sea, continuing still remorseless,' and notwithstanding her 'defect of understanding,' she is again 'ordered to be twenty-one days closely imprisoned, and (as soon as the weather will permit) dragged in the sea again after a boat, and also perform public penance in all the churches of this island.' After undergoing all this, she is apparently penitent, 'according to her capacity, 'and is ordered by the Bishop to be received into the peace of the Church, according to the forms appointed for that purpose.' 'Given under my hand this 13th day of Aug., 1720.'

Words: **"Sodor"** comes from "The Sodres" which were "The Southern Isles" of the old Norse kingdom but which we now call "The Western Isles" of Scotland; **'ware**=aware; **cherubs**=childlike angels; **unhallowed**=unholy; **mire**=mud; **tribunal**=court of three judges; **unchaste**=not pure; **incorrigible**=incurably bad; **faculty=**mental ability, aptitude; **legitimate**=lawful; **celestial**=heavenly; **temporal**=to do with earthly things; **seraph**=angel.

CATHERINE KINRADE

NONE spake when Wilson stood before
The throne—
And He that sate thereon
Spake not; and all the presence-floor
Burnt deep with blushes, as the angels cast
Their faces downwards. Then at last,
Awe-stricken, he was 'ware
How on the emerald stair
A woman sat, divinely clothed in white,
And at her knees four cherubs bright,
That laid
Their heads within her lap. Then, trembling, he essayed
To speak:—"Christ's mother, pity me!"
Then answered she:—
"Sir, I am Catherine Kinrade."

Even so—the poor dull brain,
Drenched in unhallowed fire,
It had no vigour to restrain—
God's image trodden in the mire
Of impious wrongs—whom last he saw
Gazing with animal awe

Before his harsh tribunal, proved unchaste,
Incorrigible, woman's form defaced
To uttermost ruin by no fault of hers—
So gave her to the torturers;
And now—some vital spring adjusted,
Some faculty that rusted
Cleansed to legitimate use—
Some undeveloped action stirred, some juice
Of God's distilling dropt into the core
Of all her life—no more
In that dark grave entombed,
Her soul had bloomed
To perfect woman—swift celestial growth
That mocks our temporal sloth—
To perfect woman—woman made to honour,
With all the glory of her youth upon her.
And from her lips and from her eyes there flowed
A smile that lit all Heaven; the angels smiled;
God smiled, if that were smile beneath the state that glowed
Soft purple—and a voice:—"Be reconciled!"
So to his side the children crept,
And Catherine kissed him, and he wept.
Then said a seraph:—"Lo! he is forgiven."
And for a space again there was no voice in Heaven.

LIME STREET

Here is one of Brown's many poems showing women as victims. He is walking along Lime Street in Liverpool when his eyes meet those of a prostitute who for a moment thinks Brown wants to go with her. She quickly realizes that he doesn't but is so hardened by life's knocks that she finds it hard to accept that there are some men who choose to lead pure and clean lives. The poem is stating the belief that our natural instincts are beautiful and healthy only when they are held in check by good standards and civilised behaviour. As Brown passes the woman and studies her jaded beauty, he thinks about the good influences in life which she must never have known and his pity for her is painful.

Poems like this of fourteen lines, with ten syllables in each line and the line-endings rhyming in the way Lime Street *does are known as sonnets.*

Words: burgeons=begins to grow; **Hercules**, son of Zeus, was a Greek hero with tremendous strength and an insatiable sexual appetite; **Diana** was the Roman goddess of chastity; **unblenched**=unblinking.

See also: Hotwells (p.101); Roman Women (*Collected Poems of T. E. Brown* pgs. 59 - 68).

LIME STREET

You might have been as lovely as the dawn,
Had household sweetness nurtured you, and arts
Domestic, and the strength which love imparts
To lowliness, and chastened ardour drawn
From vital sap that burgeons in the brawn
Around the dreadful arms of Hercules,
And shapes the curvature of Dian's knees,
And has its course in lilies of the lawn.
Even now your flesh is soft and full, defaced
Although it be, and bruised. Unblenched your eyes
Meet mine, as misinterpreting their call,
Then sink, reluctant, forced to recognise
That there are men whose look is not unchaste—
O God! the pain! the horror of it all!

97

GOD IS LOVE

After graduating at Oxford in 1854, T. E. Brown became an ordained deacon of the Church of England though he did not decide to become an ordained priest until thirty years later. The birth rate in Victorian times was very high but the death rate was too so no-one could go through life without knowing the grief caused by death. Most ministers felt qualified to speak with the utmost certainty of what happened to a person's soul after dying but, after a lifetime's wrestling with the scriptures and his own feelings, T. E. Brown showed no such confidence. Only three months before he died, writing to Miss Graves, a friend who did not believe in life after death, he disclosed that the Bible gave him little guidance on the subject but that, on balance, one should believe in an afterlife simply because most of the best brains in history had. To add weight in his poems to his knowledge of God's goodness (of which, of course, he had no doubts) he speaks with the authority of one who actually knows what Heaven is like. His is a very stereotyped picture with angels all over the place and seraphs and cherubs doing the Lord's business on glittering staircases as choirs sing for the rest of eternity.

Words: your angel=there is a belief that we all have a special "guardian" angel in Heaven; **say**=this might be the little girl's way of pronouncing "sea".

See also: The Prayers (p.103); Catherine Kinrade (p.94); Mater Dolorossa (p.112).

"GOD IS LOVE"

At Derby Haven in the sweet Manx land
A little girl had written in the sand
This legend:—"God is love." But, when I said:—
"What means this writing?" thus she answered:—
"It's father that's at say,
And I come here to pray,
And.....God is love." My eyes grew dim—
Blest child! in Heaven above
Your angel sees the face of Him
Whose name is love

"NE SIT ANCILLÆ"

Teignmouth (Tinmuth) is in Devon and was possibly visited by T. E. Brown when he stayed at nearby Seaton in 1881. The "British navy" Brown refers to must include fishing and merchant vessels, for Teignmouth was not a Royal Navy port.

Brown had a soft spot for women and saw them all as victims. The title, on its own, does not meaningfully translate; it is part of a fuller line (Ne sit ancillae tibi amor pudori) from one of Horace's odes which has been translated freely as "Why blush to admit that you love your slave girl?" In this poem Brown, an outwardly respectable, middle-class clergyman, is looking at a downtrodden little waitress and is "weighing her up"; judging her - something he often does though he always seems to regret it for, as Christ said, "Judge not, and ye shall be not judged". She is not Brown's slave, but she is "beneath" him in "class" and Brown, as he usually does after judging people, ends up taking a long, hard look at himself.

Words: slavey=an overworked domestic servant;   **Burton**=Burton Water (water from a spring supplying a brewery in Burton);   **sate**=sat.

"NE SIT ANCILLÆ"

Poor little Teignmouth slavey,
Squat, but rosy!
Slatternly, but cosy!
A humble adjunct of the British navy,
A fifth-rate dabbler in the British gravy—
How was I mirrored? In what spiritual dress
Appeared I to your struggling consciousness?

Thump! bump!
A dump
Of first a knife and then a fork!
Then plump
A mustard-pot! Then slump, stump, frump,
The plates
like slates—
And lastly fearful wrestling with a cork!
And so I thought:—"Poor thing!
She has not any wing
To waft her from the grease,
To give her soul release
From this dull sphere
Of baccy, beef, and beer."

99

But, as it happed,
I spoke of Chagford, Chagford by the moor,
Sweet Chagford town. Then, pure
And bright as Burton tapped
By master hand,
Then, red as is a peach,
My little maid found speech—
Gave me to understand
She knew "them parts";
And to our several hearts
We stood elate
As each revealed to each
A mate—
She stood, I sate,
And saw within her eyes
The folly of an infinite surprise.

HOTWELLS

Hotwells was the red-light district of Bristol and it is only that title which tells us that here is yet another poem about a "fallen woman". We don't know who she was nor when or where she had been known to the poet. You might find some of the imagery hard to understand; only the "shell" remaining of the original person, for instance, but Hotwells *is in this book for those of you who enjoy examining poems in detail. Once again, though, we see the pity that accompanies Brown's disgust. Although he wants this once-fair maiden to be killed, he sees that as an act of mercy and, as always, he loves the sinner even if he hates the sin.*

Words: obdurate=stubborn or hardened.

See also: Lime Street (p.97), *Roman Women* (*The Collected Poems of T. E. Brown* pgs. 59—68).

HOTWELLS

Is it her face that looks from forth the glare
Of those dull stony eyes?
Her face! that used to light with meek surprise,
If I but said that she was fair!

Can it have come to this, since at the gate
Her lips between the bars
Fluttered irresolute to mine, for it was late
Beneath the misty stars!

It was our last farewell, our last farewell—
O heaven above!
And now she is a fearful thing of Hell—
My dove! my dove!
A hollow thing carved rigid on the shell
Of her that was my love!

Yet, if the soul remain,
There crouched and dumb behind the obdurate mask,
This would I ask:—
Kill her, O God! that so, the flesh being slain,
Her soul my soul may be again.

MY GARDEN

This is, probably, the most quoted of T. E. Brown's verses, though it cannot be considered as one of his best. Sir Arthur Quiller-Couch had been a pupil at Clifton and had walked on the Downs with Brown. He became a very famous author and was editor, in 1900, of the first ever Oxford Book of English Verse; *he included* My Garden *as the only example of Brown's poetry. It might have been better for Brown's reputation if he had been left out of the volume altogether for* My Garden *has been parodied unmercifully ever since. In 1910 it appeared in a book listing, its compilers claimed, the worst one hundred poems in the English language.*

Few critics realize that it was one of several items Brown wrote for Plain Talk, *a church magazine which was produced by Brown's Baptist minister brother, Hugh Stowell Brown, a preacher in a very poor downtown area of the Liverpool docklands. He asked T. E. Brown to write something for his Sunday School's harvest festival and* My Garden *was the result.*

We shall never know if Brown considered that it was good poetry; many learned people have said that it is not. We are not even told what the "sign" is that God walks in the garden but the message seems clear enough to the many people who love this poem.

Words: wot=knows; **grot**=grotto; **is not**=does not exist; **nay**=no, why, it so happens.

MY GARDEN

A GARDEN is a lovesome thing, God wot!
Rose plot,
Fringed pool,
Ferned grot—
The veriest school
Of peace; and yet the fool
Contends that God is not—
Not God! in gardens! when the eve is cool?
Nay, but I have a sign;
'Tis very sure God walks in mine.

102

THE PRAYERS

Many people today dismiss this poem as being sloppy and sentimental - and, of course, it is. Victorian customs and beliefs encouraged sentimentality and Brown was not a revolutionary. Furthermore, this poem was not originally written for publication but was one of several written for the children of the Baptist Sunday School in Liverpool run by his brother, the Reverand Hugh Stowell Brown.

Words: presence-chamber=room where a ruler or other important person receives guests; **dight**=made ready with adornments.

See also: God is Love (p.98); Catherine Kinrade (p.94).

THE PRAYERS

I was in Heaven one day when all the prayers
Came in, and angels bore them up the stairs
    Unto a place where he
    Who was ordained such ministry
Should sort them so that in that palace bright
The presence-chamber might be duly dight;
For they were like to flowers of various bloom;
And a divinest fragrance filled the room.

Then did I see how the great sorter chose
One flower that seemed to me a hedgeling rose,
    And from the tangled press
    Of that irregular loveliness
Set it apart—and—"This," I heard him say,
"Is for the Master": so upon his way
He would have passed; then I to him:—
"Whence is this rose? O thou of cherubim
The chiefest?"—"Know'st thou not?" he said and smiled,
"This is the first prayer of a little child."

CAROL

Like all classical scholars of his time, T. E. Brown would have studied several ancient languages whilst at Christ's College. One of these would have been Early English which possibly accounts for so many archaic words appearing in his poems and also for some of the old-fashioned spellings in Carol. *He has been accused by some critics of being "rhymish" but if we examine his words carefully, we find that usually the words Brown chooses are extremely apt. You might like to think about his choice of old words and spellings in this poem.*

The story of the Epiphany, when the baby Jesus was brought gifts, is actually about "wise men" and the Bible does not mention them by name nor call them "kings"; but Carol *is a song based on the pre-Christian legend of* The Child of Wondrous Light *which was adopted by Christians, and the "Three Kings" have long been a popular part of the Christmas story.*

You and your friends might well like to compare Carol *with J. H. Hopkins's* We Three Kings of Orient Are. Carol *was set to music by J. Meredith Tatton—a master at King William's College when Brown was its Vice-Principal—and, also, later, by the renowned collector of Manx music, W. H. Gill.*

Words: withouten=without a; **dreed**=fear; **trow**=think or believe; **rouncy**=a horse, but especially a riding horse; **yclad** (ee'clad)=appropriately clothed; **dusky**=dark-skinned; **dromedar**=dromedary (one-humped camel).

CAROL

THREE kings from out the Orient
For Judah's land were fairly bent,
    To find the Lord of grace;
And as they journeyed pleasantlie;
A star kept shining in the sky,
    To guide them to the place.
"O Star," they cried, "By all confest
Withouten dreed, the loveliest!"

The first was Melchior to see,
The emperour hight of Arabye,
    An aged man, I trow;
He sat upon a rouncy bold,
Had taken of the red red gold,
    The babe for to endow.
"O Star," he cried....

104

The next was Gaspar, young and gay,
That held the realm of far Cathay—
   Our Jesus drew him thence—
Yclad in silk from head to heel,
He rode upon a high cameel,
   And bare the frankincense.
"O Star," he cried. . . .

The last was dusky Balthasar,
That rode upon a dromedar—
   His coat was of the fur.
Dark-browed he came from Samarkand,
The Christ to seek, and in his hand
   Upheld the bleeding myrrh.
"O Star," he cried, "by all confest
Withouten dreed, the loveliest.

SONG: LOOK AT ME SUN

If you love the feel of sunshine as well as its light, you will like this poem written at sunset. It is as though the sun is a person you love who is about to leave you for a while.

SONG

LOOK at me, sun, ere thou set
   In the far sea;
From the gold and the rose and the jet
   Look full at me!

Leave on my brow a trace
   Of tenderest light;
Kiss me upon the face,
   Kiss for good-night.

SONG: WEARY WIND OF THE WEST

This is a true lyric poem: it rhymes, it scans, it could be set to music for singing and it is very personal.

One can easily understand and picture the scene Brown paints with his words. It is a true "romantic" poem as it endows nature with a personality and it is also one which endorses Selwyn Simpson's remark in his book Thomas Edward Brown The Manx Poet: An Appreciation, *"...... Brown's whole treatment of Nature is tinged with a tender melancholy". The only question the poem poses is, "Who is the wind sobbing for?". Many of Brown's family and friends died during his lifetime and it is, perhaps, best if we do not suggest who is being mourned here.*

SONG

"WEARY wind of the West
　　Over the billowy sea—
Come to my heart, and rest!
　　Ah, rest with me!
Come from the distance dim
　　Bearing the sun's last sigh;
I hear thee sobbing for him
　　Through all the sky."

So the wind came,
　　Purpling the middle sea,
Crisping the ripples of flame—
　　Came unto me;
Came with a rush to the shore,
　　Came with a bound to the hill,
Fell, and died at my feet—
　　Then all was still.

106

OH! FATHER'S AT SEA

This poem was obviously written to be sung. It does not appear in The Collected Poems of T. E. Brown *but was published in 1915 in* Lullabies of the Four Nations, *compiled by Adelaide L. J. Gosset. Brown was an accomplished musician but if he wrote a tune for this song, it hasn't survived so, perhaps, you should write one.*

Words: likely=probably.

See also: Mater Dolorosa (p.112).

OH! FATHER'S AT SEA

Oh! father's at the sea, little baby mine,
Oh! father's at the sea, little baby mine;
And you are all I've got, here a-sleepin' in your cot,
Such a blessed little dot, little baby mine!

Oh, he's never seen you yet, little baby mine,
Oh, he's never seen you yet, little baby mine;
And you are all I've got, here a-sleepin' in your cot,
Such a blessed little dot, little haby mine!

But when he comes at last, little baby mine,
Oh, when he comes at last, little baby mine,
I' hide you here in bed - Oh, the pretty little head!
And nothing'll be said, little baby mine!

Then I'll turn down the sheet, little baby mine;
Oh! I'll turn down the sheet, little baby mine;
The sheet as white as snow, with a ho! ho! ho! ho! ho!
And then I'll let him know, little baby mine!

And then you'll laugh and coo, little baby mine,
And then you'll laugh and coo, little baby mine;
And then he'll say, "What's this?" and likely, "Not amiss,"
And then he'll kiss and kiss little baby mine!

And you as good as gold, little baby mine,
Oh, you as good as gold, little baby mine;
O howling, howling sea, as quick as quick can be,
Send my Billy back to me and to this baby mine!

ON   BRADDA'S   HEIGHTS

This is not in The Collected Poems *but is found in several books about Brown. It was written when he was young, before Milner's Tower was errected on Bradda but whilst the copper and lead mines were still active. The poem was never completed and Brown did not have it published; the words in brackets are the alternatives he was considering. The theme is one found in works by many poets - the smallness of mankind compared with the magnitude of "nature" and the briefness of man's life compared with eternity. The personification of the cliffs and waves reveals that the romantic view of nature, which he shows in his later poems, had existed from a very early age.*

Words: quaffed=drunk in big gulps;   **cords**=chords;   **despot**=dictator;   **annals**=records; **graven**=engraved, carved;   **iron pen**=probably refers to the iron and steel miners' tools; **hoar**=grey [haired] with age;   **circling spheres**=planets.

ON   BRADDA'S   HEIGHTS

"On Bradda's heights I took my stand
   And watched the blue waves as they toiled below,
And saw how they bounded upon the strand
   And bent their proud crests of the riven snow.

Onward they came, and one by one
   Flat on the sounding beach they fell.
And others sprang up at their dying groan
   And wildly they rang the funeral knell.

And ever as died a weary wave,
   On the welcome couch of the pebbly shore,
Another swept o'er the new made grave,
   And held the place that he had held before.

'Oh! such the fate of Man,' I cried.
  Roughly he rolls on Time's wide sea,
And borne on the rush of the running tide,
  Breaks on the shore of Eternity.

And another laughs, where he hath laughed,
  And another weeps, where he hath wept;
And the golden bowl of Life is quaffed,
  And the silvery cords of his harp have slept.

Away the mist from off the gloomy brow,
  Proud Bradda, rival of the wrestling [wreckless] storm,
Tear from the mossy [lofty] head the cloud-cap now,
  And give me all revealed thy giant form.

Lord of the tempest - despot of the wave -
  That dies, its white teeth gnashing at thy feet,
Art thou the stone that marks the ages' grave
  Reared by some mighty hand in Time's wide street.

Yea! I can read [trace] the annals of the Past
   Graven on thy bare breast with an iron pen,
That trembled in the fingers of the blast,
   And wrote of times that were - that ne'er shall be again.

And while I gaze upon thy summit hoar
   That tow'rs as though to seek some other clime,
With thee my trembling spirit seems to soar,
   And hears soft echoes of the olden Time.

But thou shalt last, and when the weary years
   Have sought the bosom of Eternity,
And borne me far beyond the circling spheres,
   Thou shalt look on, proud cliff, unmovedly.
Ay! when this dust the earth-worms' food shall be
Thou still shall stand and frown along the heaving sea."

JUVENTA PERENNIS

[Eternal Youth]

To drink the "wine of youth" is another way of saying "enjoy yourself while you're young".
But Brown says here, "hold up the cup for some more of life's enjoyment, even when you are old".

JUVENTA PERENNIS

If youth be thine,
Spare not to drink its wine;
If youth be fled,
Hold up
The golden cup—
God's grapes are always red.

VESPERS

What one person enjoys doing is sometimes seen by others as a waste of time. Brown's little poem brings to mind many epithets and proverbs such as "One man's meat is another man's poison" or the debate which must have gone on from the beginning of civilization highlighted by the poet Thomas Gray (1716-1771) when he wrote, "that where ignorance is bliss, 'tis folly to be wise".

It is worth reading Vespers *many times to appreciate Brown's observations and thoughts. Do you think, for instance, that the title forms an important part of the whole work?*

Words: **Vespers**=the sixth of seven named hours of evening prayers; commonly nowadays, simply, "evening prayers"; **saith**(seth)=says.

VESPERS

O BLACKBIRD, what a boy you are!
How you do go it!
Blowing your bugle to that one sweet star—
How you do blow it!
And does she hear you, blackbird boy, so far?
Or is it wasted breath?
"Good Lord! she is so bright
To-night!"
The blackbird saith.

MATER DOLOROSA
[Grief striken mother]

In *Victorian times when these poems were written and cures for illnesses were not so certain, it was quite common for babies and young children to die from ailments which today can be successfully treated; but the loss of any infant must have been just as distressing for the relatives then as it is now. Billy has returned to a tragedy and his wife, the once excited young mother who sang* Oh! Father's at Sea *(p.107), cries her sorrow for him and herself as she tries to gain comfort from the belief that dead babies go to Heaven to be nursed by angels.*

The title is from the opening couplet "Stabat mater dolorosa juxta crucem lacrimosa" which was written by the thirteenth-century Franciscan, Jacopone da Todi, and means "The grief-stricken mother was standing in tears by the cross".

Words: nuss= nurse; **bress**=breast; **pessin**=person; **Illiam**=William (Billy).

See also: Going to meet him (In the coach) (p.39); The Christening (p.15).

MATER DOLOROSA

Aw, Billy, good sowl! don't cuss! don't cuss!
Ye see, these angels is grand to nuss;
And it's lek they're feedin' them on some nice air,
Or dew or the lek, that's handy there,
O Billy, look at my poor poor bress!
O Billy, see the full it is!
But . . . O my God! . . . but navar mind!
There's no doubt them sperrits is very kind—
And of coorse they're that beautiful it's lekly
The childher is takin' to them directly—
Eh, Billy, eh? . . . And . . . O my head!
Billy, Billy, come to bed! . . .
And the little things that navar knew sin—
And everything as nate as a pin
And the lovely bells goin' ding-a-lingin'—
And of coorse we've allis heard of their singin'.
But won't he want me when he'll be wakin'?

Will they take him up when he's wantin' takin'?
I hope he'll not be left in the dark—
He was allis used to make a wark
If a body'd lave him the smallest minute—
Dear me! the little linnet—
But I forgot—it's allis light
In yandhar place . . . All right! all right!
I forgot, ye see, . . . I'm not very well . . .
Light, was I sayin'? but who can tell?
Bad for the eyes, though . . . but a little curtain
On a string, ye know—aw certain! certain!
Let me feel your face, Billy! Jus' us two!
Aw, Billy, the sorry I am for you!
Aw 'deed it is, Billy,—very disthressin'
To lave your childher to another pessin—
But . . . all the little rooms that's theer—
And Jesus walkin' up the steer,
And tappin' lek—I see! I see!—
O Jesus Christ, have pity on me!
But He'll come, He'll come! He'll give a look
Jus' to see the care that's took—
O! there's no doubt He's very gud—
I think He wud, I think He wud!
But still . . . but still . . . but I don't know . . .
Billy! I think I'd like to go—
What's that, Billy? did ye hear a cry?
Illiam, the sweet it'd be to die!

113

EX ORE INFANTIS
(Out of the mouth of a babe)

This poem was founded on a story sent to Brown by his friend Miss Graves. She frequently discussed life after death with Brown and he responded to the story with this then untitled poem. After Brown's death, Miss Graves presented the poem to the editors of The Collected Poems of T. E. Brown *and they gave it its title which is an adaptation by them of a verse in* Psalm 8: *(Out of the mouths of babes and sucklings thou has perfected praise). The sad poems about death in this book portray the intensity of human suffering and they reveal both Brown's experience and his compassion. Right up to the time he, himself, died, Brown found it difficult to see any divine purpose in the pain of separation caused by death, or to come to terms with the conventional certainties expressed by church ministers which were supposed to comfort people when their loved ones died. This poem attempts to offer hope that a better life immediately follows death. This is tendered as a crumb of comfort to the grieving mother.*

Words: converted=(note the italics) someone is asking the poet, "Was the mother converted?" i.e. a born-again Christian, a believer; **creed**=basic fundamental beliefs; **lenten**=as small a quantity as one would have when fasting in Lent.

EX ORE INFANTIS

HER husband died before her babe was born
Two years ago. *Converted?* Doubt and grief,
Poor soul! she felt. Her Methodist creed forlorn
Gave but a lenten substance of relief.
To-day, beneath the piteous gaze of morn,
Her child is dying. On his little brow
Descends the veil, and all is over now—
Not yet! not yet! For suddenly he springs,
As who perceived the gleam of golden wings.
"Dada!" he cries, he knows his father's face
Ne'er seen before. O God, Thou giv'st the grace!
O widowed heart! They live in Heaven's fair light,
Your husband with his boy. The child was right.

WHEN LOVE MEETS LOVE

The conventional belief in Brown's day was that God chose the moment for people to die and here Brown is agonising over the death of a child. The poem was written on Brown's 48th birthday, just over two years after his son, Braddan, died of diptheria, aged just seven. This is one of several of Brown's poems asking "What is life all about?". A child is created through love but when God takes the fruit of that love, "Where is all our love?", he asks.

WHEN LOVE MEETS LOVE

WHEN love meets love, breast urged to breast,
God interposes,
An unacknowledged guest,
And leaves a little child among our roses.
O, gentle hap!
O, sacred lap!
O, brooding dove!
But when he grows
Himself to be a rose,
God takes him—where is then our love?
O, where is all our love?

BETWEEN OUR FOLDING LIPS

This poem was written on the day after When Love Meets Love. *Although death is not mentioned here, the imagery is the same in both poems, and one has to wonder if Brown is attempting to find a satisfactory answer to the question he asked the day before.*

BETWEEN OUR FOLDING LIPS

BETWEEN our folding lips
God slips
An embryon of life, and goes;
And this becomes your rose.
We love, God makes: in our sweet mirth
God spies occasion for a birth.
Then is it His, or is it ours?
I know not—He is fond of flowers.

THE SCHOONER

This is considered by many people to be one of Brown's finest works. You can simply read it and enjoy the pictures and changes of mood the poet has created or you can search to see how these have been achieved. You might even like to discuss whether or not it is a lyrical poem.

Brown has crafted the words very carefully to produce the energy and tensions which make the poem special; the repeated use of "and" reinforces the messages his words give, alliteration highlights the actions and effects he is illustrating and by introducing soft, gentle words, he achieves the contrast which is the essence of the poem. Is this simply a poem about a schooner or do you think that there are hidden meanings?

Words: schooner=a fore and aft rigged sailing vessel with two or more masts; **hoggish**=like a fat pig; **crapulous**=drunken; **viragoes**=tough women; **tiller**=handle of a rudder; **canvas**=a sail or sails; **bowsprit**= spar projecting from ship's bow to carry stays for the most forward sails; **gunwale** (gunnel)="gun-wall", upper edge of a ship's side; **bilge**=space under the lowest floorings of a ship where dirt and foul water collects; **draught**=literally, the depth of a boat below the waterline; **transverse**=horizontal line, the horizon; **throes**=violent disturbances (physical or mental); **benediction**=blessing; **methinks**= I think.

THE SCHOONER

JUST mark that schooner westward far at sea—
    'Tis but an hour ago
When she was lying hoggish at the quay,
    And men ran to and fro,
And tugged, and stamped, and shoved, and pushed, and swore,
And ever and anon, with crapulous glee,
Grinned homage to viragoes on the shore.

So to the jetty gradual she was hauled:
    Then one the tiller took,
And chewed, and spat upon his hand, and bawled;
    And one the canvas shook
Forth like a mouldy bat; and one, with nods
And smiles, lay on the bowsprit-end, and called
And cursed the Harbour-master by his gods.

And, rotten from the gunwale to the keel,
    Rat-riddled, bilge-bestank,
Slime-slobbered, horrible, I saw her reel,
    And drag her oozy flank,

116

And sprawl among the deft young waves, that laughed,
And leapt, and turned in many a sportive wheel,
As she thumped onward with her lumbering draught.

And now, behold! a shadow of repose
    Upon a line of gray,
She sleeps, that transverse cuts the evening rose—
She sleeps, and dreams away,
Soft-blended in a unity of rest
All jars, and strifes obscene, and turbulent throes
'Neath the broad benediction of the West—

Sleeps; and methinks she changes as she sleeps,
    And dies, and is a spirit pure.
Lo! on her deck an angel pilot keeps
    His lonely watch secure;
And at the entrance of Heaven's dockyard waits,
Till from Night's leash the fine-breath'd morning leaps,
And that strong hand within unbars the gates.

FIVES'-COURT

Fives was a very popular game at boarding schools and universities. It is played on a much smaller version of a squash court and instead of a racket, players propel the ball with their gloved hand. Like much poetry, this one of Brown's is not about the subject of its title; it is a sad, reflective verse where the court is supposedly endowed with life and the ability to preserve lingering memories. The nub of the poem is contained in the rhetorical question (one which does not require an answer) posed in the last two lines.

Words: langsyne=long since (Lowland Scottish).

See also: Not Willing to Stay (p.92).

FIVES'-COURT

SOMETIMES at night I stand within a court
    Where I have play'd by day;
And still the walls are vibrant with the sport,
    And still the air is pulsing with the sway
      Of agile limbs that now, their labours o'er,
To healthful sleep their strength resign—
But how of those who play'd with me langsyne,
And sleep for evermore?

PLANTING

Many people feel that poems cannot successfully be read silently and only really come to life when shared with an audience; but this is a very private, personal poem and each listener or reader will have a private and personal perception of any meaning it might have. It ends with a clearly defined wish but what is the nature of the wish? Is it life or is it death which is on Brown's mind and is it his body, his soul or his life which he asks be planted?

Words: guerdon=reward, recompense;   **coil**=disturbance, turmoil;   **arbitrate**=negotiate;
foil=background;   **meet**=suitable;   **skills**=matters.

PLANTING

WHO would be planted chooseth not the soil,
Or here or there,
Or loam or peat,
Wherein he best may grow,
And bring forth guerdon of the planter's toil—
The lily is most fair,
But says not:—"I will only blow
Upon a southern land"; the cedar makes no coil
What rock shall owe
The springs that wash his feet;
The crocus cannot arbitrate the foil
That for its purple radiance is most meet—
Lord, even so
I ask one prayer,
The which if it be granted,
It skills not where
Thou plantest me, only I would be planted.

ALMA MATER
(Bounteous Mother)

Brown held contradictory views about the nature of an afterlife and in Alma Mater *the doubts which were part of his innermost thoughts are openly revealed. The poem illustrates a confusion of ideas which are still current today. Does the soul take flight after death and, if so, by what mechanism does it travel? ... and to where? Brown's writings show how close he felt to nature, and several commentators have described him as a pantheist; in Alma Mater he is stating that he loves Earth too much for there to be any attraction in the lifting of his soul to a higher plane after death.*

Brown has possibly taken the title from the works of the Roman poet, Lucretius, who wrote " .... all have the same father, from whom, when our fostering mother earth has received liquid drops of water ..." but alma comes from alo which means "I nourish" and amongst the many acceptable translations of the words Alma Mater *has to be "mother Earth" which occurs throughout this poem. The only surviving use of this phrase is as a means of referring to one's old school or university.*

Words: conic sections=angular sections through a cone expressing, mathematically, the idea of different planes; **Daedalus**=In Greek Mythology he built a pair of wings for himself and a pair for his son, Icarus, so that they could escape from their employer, King Minos of Crete. Icarus flew too near the sun; the wax holding the feathers to the wings melted and Icarus crashed to the sea. **quiddities**=quibbles, argumentative interpretations of meanings; **novercae**=stepmothers (here it means wicked stepmothers).

See also: Epistola ad Dakyns (p.77).

ALMA MATER
(Bounteous Mother)

O mother Earth, by the bright sky above thee,
I love thee, O, I love thee!
And yet they say that I must leave thee soon;
    And if it must be so,
Then to what sun or moon
    Or star I am to go,
    Or planet, matters not for me to know.
O mother Earth, by the bright sky above thee,
I love thee, O I love thee!

O? whither will you send mc?
O, wherefore will you rend me
 From your warm bosom, mother mine?—
I can't fix my affections
On a state of conic sections,
And I don't care how old Daedalus
May try to coax and wheedle us
With wings he manufactures,
Sure to end in compound fractures,
 Or in headers at right-angles to the brine—
O mother Earth, by the bright sky above thee,
I love thee, O, I love thee!
 I cannot leave thee, mother:
 I love thee, and not another;
 And I can't say "man and brother"
 To a shadowy abstraction,
 To an uncomfortable fraction,
 To the skeletons of quiddities,
 And similar stupidities.
 Have mercy, mother, mercy!
 The unjustest of *novercae*
 Sometimes leaves off her snarlings
 At her predecessor's darlings;
 And thou art *all* my mother,
 I know not any other.

O mother Earth, by the bright sky above thee,
I love thee, O, I love thee!

So let me leave thee never,
But cling to thee for ever,
And hover round thy mountains,
And flutter round thy fountains,
 And pry into thy roses fresh and red;
And blush in all thy blushes,
And flush in all thy flushes,
And watch when thou art sleeping,

And weep when thou art weeping,
And be carried with thy motion,
As the rivers and the ocean,
As the great rocks and the trees are,
And all the things one sees are—
O mother, this were glorious life,
    This were not to be dead.
O mother Earth, by the bright sky above thee,
I love thee, O, I love thee!

AT THE PLAY

Although this is another poem which refers to death, it is a very beautiful and finely crafted sonnet. It is the last work in The Collected Poems of T. E. Brown *and a fitting one to end this small selection.*

Almost everyone ponders at some time or other what life is "all about" and here Brown imbues it with the illusory characteristics of a theatrical play. But whether we see ourselves as actors or audience in life's pageant, when our time comes to die, we cannot say, "No, thank you very much, I think I'll come back for tomorrow's performance instead." Could At the Play, *perhaps, have inspired the person who first coined the phrase "Life is not a dress-rehearsal"?*

Words: vicissitudes=difficulties in achieving an objective; **Damon**=a shepherd singer in one of Virgil's plays—also a name given by poets to any rustic, male lover; **motley**=colourful costume worn by fools and jesters, though here it simply means colour or brightness; **acme** (ack-mee)=sublime peak; **lights gutter**=the flickering of oil footlamps as they run out of fuel; **o'er-watched varlets**=(theatre) staff who have watched the play so many times that they are weary of it; **intimãte**=indirectly suggest; **adumbrãte**=foreshadowed, faintly or obscurely outlined; **specious** (spee-she-us)= appearing to be true though actually false.

121

AT THE PLAY

As in a theatre the amuséd sense
Beholds the strange vicissitudes of things,
Young Damon's loves, the fates of clowns and kings,
And all the motley of the gay pretence—
Beholds, and on an acme of suspense
Stands vibrant till the curtain falls, door swings,
Lights gutter, and the weary murmurings
Of o'er-watched varlets intimate us thence:
Even so we gaze not on the things that are,
Nor aught behold but what is adumbrate.
The show is specious, and we laugh and weep
At what is only meant spectacular;
And when the curtain falls, we may not wait:
Death takes the lights, and we go home to sleep.

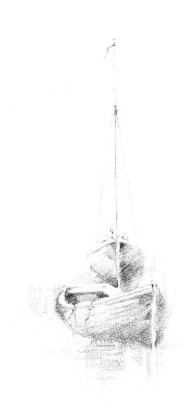